The Local Government Service

First Published in 1952, *The Local Government Service* describes in general terms the character and extent of the tasks which the body of public servants employed by the local authorities is called upon to perform. Part I comprises a general survey; Part II studies in greater detail the character and work of the agencies which are shaping the service today- the organizations of employers and staff, the Whitley machinery, and the local authority in its capacity as an individual employer; while Part III deals with the more important aspects and issues of qualification and training in a way which could not have been attempted in part I without impeding the narrative.

This is a must read for students of public administration and political science.

The Local Government Service

J.H. Warren

Routledge
Taylor & Francis Group

First published in 1952
by George Allen & Unwin Ltd.

This edition first published in 2024 by Routledge
4 Park Square, Milton Park, Abingdon, Oxon, OX14 4RN

and by Routledge
605 Third Avenue, New York, NY 10017

Routledge is an imprint of the Taylor & Francis Group, an informa business

Publisher's Note
The publisher has gone to great lengths to ensure the quality of this reprint but points out that some imperfections in the original copies may be apparent.

Disclaimer
The publisher has made every effort to trace copyright holders and welcomes correspondence from those they have been unable to contact.

A Library of Congress record exists under LCCN: 52003442

ISBN: 978-1-032-85990-3 (hbk)
ISBN: 978-1-003-52080-1 (ebk)
ISBN: 978-1-032-85991-0 (pbk)

Book DOI 10.4324/9781003520801

THE LOCAL GOVERNMENT SERVICE

by

J. H. WARREN

M.A., D.P.A., Solicitor

General Secretary, National Association of Local Government Officers
Formerly Town Clerk, Slough
Sometime External Lecturer in Public Administration
University of Liverpool
Author of
'Municipal Trading'
'The English Local Government System'
'Municipal Administration'

———

GEORGE ALLEN & UNWIN LTD
Museum Street London

FIRST PUBLISHED IN 1952

PRINTED IN GREAT BRITAIN
in 11 point Baskerville type
BY PURNELL AND SONS, LTD.
PAULTON (SOMERSET) AND LONDON

Introduction

THE SUBJECT of this book is sufficiently indicated by its title
'The Local Government Service', if this be recognized as an
appellation. It is, in fact, the appellation now quite commonly applied to that body of public servants which is comprised of the paid officers employed by our Local Authorities.
Not all the employees of our Local Authorities are 'officers'.
The usage of the term does not extend to manual workers;
and manual workers in Local Authority employ are not
usually thought of as included in the Local Government
Service. Nor indeed are the school-teachers engaged in the
public education service, or the police, despite the fact that
the former are employees of the Local Authorities, and that
the latter, if not employees of the Local Authorities in a
strict legal sense, are wholly or partly under their control.
Teachers and policemen, in fact, are usually thought of as
belonging to separate and well-defined services of their own.
Broadly speaking, the employees who fall within the denotation of the term 'officer', who are generally described as
Local Government Officers, and who constitute the Local
Government Service, are those who participate in the
administration and management of Local Authority services,
and whose duties are of an administrative, professional,
technical, or clerical nature.

The purpose of the following pages is to describe in general
terms the character and extent of the tasks which this body
of public servants is called upon to perform; to survey its
composition; to trace the developments which have brought
about national standards of qualification, conduct, and
employment such as to stamp a congeries of locally appointed
employees with the character of a national service; to describe and discuss these standards in relation to the requirements of efficient service to the nation; to indicate the
agencies which now shape the Service and to explain how
these work; and, not least in importance, to show in what

relationship Local Government officers stand, in our political system, to their employers, the Local Authorities, and to the citizens to whose needs they minister.

The subject matter thus indicated has quite obviously a potential interest of many varied kinds, dependent upon the reader's approach as much as the author's. A compendious treatment of 'pay and conditions' could be relied upon to elicit a very personal interest on the part of officers themselves, and might provide a useful digest for reference by councillors. The social statistician might find something of interest in a survey of the Local Government Service as a field of occupation. The educationist might find interest in the requirements of the Service in matters of qualification and training. Parents, school teachers, and those Civil Servants who are concerned with the choice of employment, might look for information as to the careers the Service offers.

It is, however, no part of the author's aim to write a manual of service conditions, or a guide to careers, or indeed to cater for any interests quite so personal or special as those we have mentioned, though the book may communicate incidentally some information of value to those who approach it with these interests predominant.

The members of Local Authorities and the personnel of the Local Government Service itself do, however, constitute a class of reader to whose special interests the author has addressed himself consistently with his general aim. The settlement of many if not most of the service conditions of Local Government officers by a process of collective bargaining through Whitley machinery, and the progressive establishment through Whitley machinery and other agencies of standards of qualification and conduct to which officers are required to conform, both of them processes which have developed in recent years, have no doubt eased in many respects the task of the individual Local Authority in the selection and management of its staff. But the members of a Local Authority still need an understanding of the essential nature of these processes, and of the Whitley machinery through which they are carried out, and, on the other hand, a realization of the functions which still fall to

the Local Authority itself in the control and management of
its staff. A similar understanding is called for on the part of
the staffs, who, through the participation of their representatives, as well as those of the employers, in the Whitley
machinery, have been brought into a relationship with their
employers, in the matter of service conditions, very different
from what it was years ago. Questions of education and
training are likewise of mutual concern to both members and
officers of our Local Authorities; and, indeed, many of these
questions, as we shall see, are now dealt with by the Whitley
machinery. In fact, the whole task of personnel management
in Local Authority administration—a task which itself
engages the attention of specialized Local Government
officers in some localities—has in recent years been placed
on an entirely new footing. With these circumstances in
mind, the book has been designed to help Local Authority
personnel towards an understanding of recent developments,
and a knowledge of the machinery and procedure of Whitleyism—topics on which little has found its way into print,
and then only in scattered sources.

Primarily, however, these pages are designed for the
'general reader'. They envisage the Local Government
Service as an instrument of public service—an instrument in
the hands of the elected representatives of the people for the
achievement of those tasks of government, and of service to
the public, which fall to the responsibility of Local Authorities under our British system of Local Government. They aim
at a description, and to some extent an appraisal, of this
instrument, in relation to the uses to which it is put, and the
ends it is designed to serve. They are relevant, therefore, to
a wide variety of studies in the field of social and political
science, but, above all, to the interests of the reader as an
ordinary citizen, in that they study an agency which is
indispensable to his daily life. Their topic is important in the
measure that Local Government is important, for in modern
conditions the efficiency of Local Government is obviously
dependent on that of the Local Government Service.

Of the importance of Local Government there can surely
be no question. It is manifest when we consider the range,

the character, and the impact upon the daily life of the citizen, of the functions which our Local Authorities carry out. It is only a fraction of these which are functions of government in the older sense of the term; that is to say, restraints of a regulative character imposed upon the individual in the interests of all. By far the greater portion of them take the form of *services*, supplying economic wants of an indispensable character or providing amenities which we are very thankful to have. The protection of the police, the services of the fire brigade, the provision and maintenance of roads and streets, the multiple forms of sanitation such as sewering, sewage disposal, refuse collection, street lighting and cleansing, and the supply of water, are all of them services of an economic character which we could not do without. If these services were suddenly to cease, we should relapse into barbarism. If they are not all 'productive', in the narrow sense sometimes given to this term in economic discussions, they are often more important than some fields of productive industry, in that they establish the essential conditions for production of every kind. This is true even of a Local Authority service such as education. Modern industry cannot be carried on by an uneducated nation.

The functions and services we have cited are only examples chosen at random. In the next chapter we shall show just how wide the range of Local Authority services is, how many economic wants it supplies in the daily life of the citizen, how many of the activities of the Welfare State have been pioneered by Local Government, and how important still is that sector of social need and economic want which is catered for by Local Government. We shall illustrate the heavy financial responsibility and the complex administrative task which Local Government sustains.

It would, however, be a mistake to assess the importance of Local Government purely in terms of the services which it provides to-day, or those which it pioneered throughout the last century, and may in some instances have lost to State agencies after 1945. It is obvious that, to-day, Local Government is no longer what it was throughout the nineteenth century and the first twenty-five years of the twentieth, namely, the sole available agency, with the exception of the Post Office, for the conduct of civil public services. The development of the modern Civil Service, the ability of the modern State to enlist the services of directing and managing personnel who become the prototypes, in the sphere of public service, of the industrial and commercial entrepreneur, have made both the Government Department and the Public Corporation (in its many variant forms) an alternative agency for the conduct of public services. Both of these new agencies were resorted to even in the period between the two wars, when Local Government was doing so much in the development of the social services. Since 1945, one or the other has in many instances been preferred to Local Government for the conduct of new or transformed services, or has displaced Local Authority responsibility as well as 'private enterprise' in the conduct of longstanding 'public utility' services, such as the supply of electricity and gas. In the wider choice now open, a larger variety of considerations must necessarily enter into the choice of agency for a particular public service than before. Amenability to national planning, uniformity of practice, integration of policy, control, and administration—all these must be considered. And, for some services, the other agencies may, on a balance of considerations, be deemed more suitable than Local Government.

It must nevertheless be said with emphasis that if we adhere to all that is vital and uncontroversial in British political thinking, Local Government is not merely to be conceived of as one of several convenient agencies for the administration of public services. Its rôle must be conceived of on grounds of political principle, not merely administrative expediency. Its place in our constitution belongs to our conception of the democratic state. This conception implies representative institutions at the local as well as the central level, with an ample measure of free responsibility at the local level for appropriate sectors of governance, social provision, and public service. Local self-government at the local level must be conceived of as a permanent and standing institution which at all times and in all circumstances provides an ample repository of local power. It should ever be accorded a first preference in our mental approach to the choice of administrative agency for any service in which organization on a local basis is a necessary element.

Fully to expound these propositions would involve a deep analysis of the texture of English political thought, but the broad considerations on which they are founded are not far to seek. A vigorous Local Government is a constitutional check and balance of a practical kind, and there is no less need of this kind of constitutional device to-day than at any time in the past. It is a safeguard against the undue extension of the bureaucratic arm of the State and the power of its central executive. Above everything, however, Local Government is a fundamental institution because of its educative effect upon the mass of ordinary citizens. Not only can the actual processes of government be more fully and closely observed on the local than on the central plane by the citizens who take no active part in them. What is more important still is the extent to which Local Government draws ordinary citizens into actual participation in the process of government. No form of political education can be better than this, and no democratic State can ultimately dispense with it. In the last analysis the stability and resiliency of a democratic State must depend on a leaven of ordinary citizens who have developed political capacity by the exercise of active political responsibility, and who remain in close touch with their fellows.

The conception just put forward, of the rôle and importance of Local Government in the democratic State, is one which makes its own ideal demands upon each main aspect of a Local Government system. The structure of Local Government, its finance, the constitution of the Local Authority itself, should all be such as to give real responsibility to the elected representatives and such as to preserve the closest links between them and the electorate, so that, on the one hand, the exercise of responsibility is made visible, and, on the other hand, the fullest opportunity is available to educate popular judgment on local tasks and issues.

With the Local Government system in general this book is not concerned, and the reader must turn to other books in this series if he wishes to learn something of its main features. There is, however, one corollary of the principle that elected representatives should exercise a real responsibility which is closely relevant to our theme, i.e. that the elected Council should exercise a full authority over its officers. There have been, and still are, systems of Local Government in which the power of the official is too great, in which he has been given independent responsibilities for administration, without responsibility to the elected Council, but often, indeed, with responsibility to the central organs of the State. There are systems in which his powers go further, and he exercises a certain control over policy, either conferred by law, or assumed in a climate of political thought favourable to such a development.

In the conception of Local Government which we have put forward there is no place for the *control* of policy by the official. It is essential to democratic efficiency that the elected bodies should make full use of his knowledge and abilities, and take his advice and suggestions into account in the process of forming policy, but the control of policy must remain with the elected representatives.

In a study of the Local Government Service mainly written from the standpoint now indicated, and in which the Local Government Service is visualized as a constituent part of the Local Government system, the constitutional relationships between the officer and his employing council are a necessary and important topic in a variety of contexts. In particular, however, these relationships will be studied in the light of the conception of Local Government put forward, and brought to the test of its inherent principles.

To summarize and conclude, two aims have been continually in mind in the writing of these pages. First, to survey the Local Government Service, and to discuss its characteristics, with reference to the requirements of efficiency made upon it for the purposes for which it is established; and, secondly, to throw into clear relief its relationships with the citizens and their elected representatives.

Part I comprises a general survey; Part II studies in greater detail the character and work of the agencies which are shaping the Service to-day—the organizations of employers and staff, the Whitley machinery, and the Local Authority in its capacity as an individual employer; while Part III deals with the more important aspects and issues of Qualification and Training in a way which could not have been attempted in Part I without impeding the narrative.

CONTENTS

xiv
CONTENTS

PART II

THE SHAPING AGENCIES

PART III

QUALIFICATIONS AND TRAINING

PART ONE

THE SERVICE DESCRIBED

CHAPTER I

Tasks and Achievements

OUR SYSTEM of Local Government would not be what it is if the Local Government Service could claim the whole credit and responsibility for the work and achievements of British Local Government. Any such claim would be wide of the truth. Yet the tasks of the Service reflect the tasks of Local Government, and a broad assessment of them must necessarily be based on a general view of the scale and content of Local Government activities.

Only in comparatively recent years has the public realised the extent to which these activities have grown, or the width of their impacts upon the daily life of the citizen; and even to-day it appreciates only inadequately the part which Local Government has played in social and economic development since we entered some one hundred and fifty years ago on that phase of our civilization introduced by the Industrial Revolution. No social historian has taken up the story told by the Webbs in their classic histories of Local Government up to the Municipal Corporations Act of 1835, by treating on the same monumental scale the development of modern Local Government from those beginnings where the Webbs ended. Professor Redlich, in his notable treatise on *Local Government in England*, published in 1899, indicated its functions as they then stood, but was mainly concerned with its spirit and form, from a political and constitutional standpoint. The symposium on *A Century of Municipal Progress*, which appeared in 1935 under the joint editorship of Harold Laski, W. Ivor Jennings and W. A. Robson, presented as full a history of the modern period as had yet then appeared. Quite recently K. B. Smellie has provided an admirable short conspectus in his volume *A History of Local Government* in this series. And the writer of these lines has summarized developments between the two wars, and the great changes since the conclusion of the Second World War, in his chapter on Local Government in the symposium *British Government Since* 1918, published in 1950. But all these together hardly present a full and connected story. The rapidity of development and the cumulative enlargement of the field have outstripped the specialist historian.

It is safe to say that the full story when written will prove to be an astonishing one. It will show how largely the foundations of what is now called 'the welfare state' were laid by Local Government, and how largely, indeed, the system of industrial production which we call private enterprise was dependent upon communal services undertaken by Local Authorities. It will show to what extent the services now carried out by other agencies such as Public Corporations have been pioneered by Local Government; and to what extent all classes of the community, and some classes in particular, must still rely on the Local Authority's daily ministrations for many of the essentials of civilized life and for not a few of its amenities.

Daily Ministrations

For the proof and illustration of these propositions the reader must be referred to other works, including those cited, but there is one short illustration which the author may repeat from a work of his own. Writing in 1944, just before the close of the war, he sketched the normal peace-time impact of Local Government on the daily life of the citizen in the following terms:

'Let us illustrate the situation by following the successive phases of an average citizen's life and seeing how Local Government ministers to him in them all. It begins to do so before he is born, his pre-natal welfare, and the care of his mother, being the concern of the Local Authority's Maternity and Child Welfare Service. At birth, both mother and child may be cared for by its Midwifery Service. For two years after birth the child continues to have some measure of help, at post-natal clinics, from the Maternity and Child Welfare Service. In the succeeding three years, and before the child attains the age for scholastic education, he may attend a Nursery School associated with the Education

Service. At five years of age he passes into the care of the Local Authority's Education Service for scholastic education; and may so remain until he leaves school at 15, or undergoes some form of secondary education until the age of 16, 17, or even 18. During the first school years the Education Service may, in circumstances of necessity, provide him with clothes and boots, and it will extend to him, as a matter of course, school meals, medical examination, and a measure of medical care, the latter including dental, optical, and orthopaedic treatment. At school, he will be provided with recreational facilities in gymnasia, baths, or playing fields attached to the school, apart from any use he may make of similar facilities provided by the Local Authority for the general public in parks, recreation grounds, and open spaces.

'When the child passes into employment, the Local Authority will still continue to extend the help of its Education and Health Services. These may continue to furnish him with technical instruction or cultural education in part-time Continuation Schools, Young People's Colleges, or classes run by voluntary bodies such as the Workers' Educational Association with the Local Authority's help; or with medical treatment at a Municipal General Hospital, or at clinics, sanatoria, isolation hospitals or similar institutions for the treatment of special diseases such as tuberculosis and the infectious fevers.

'During all this time the child's parental home may be a council house provided by the Local Authority under the Housing Acts; and whether this be so or not, the home will be provided with at least one service by the Local Authority, namely sewerage, and it is more than likely that the Local Authority will also be supplying it with gas, electricity, and water. When the child grows up and marries it may again be the Local Authority which provides him with a dwelling-house, and most of the services mentioned.

'Day by day, throughout his life, he will move in and among streets, houses, shops, factories, offices, churches, schools, and places of amusement, the building of which has been regulated by the Local Authority under the Public Health code and the by-laws relating to new streets and buildings, and either in accordance with modern planning ideals, or at least in a conscious desire to mitigate the ugly congestion and squalor left behind by the early industrial age. In his passage along the streets he will often be conveyed by the municipality's buses, trams, or trackless trolley vehicles.

'All this aggregate of "building development", as it is called, will be protected, as also will the lives and property of the citizens at large, by the Local Authority's Police and Fire Protection Services, and maintained in a sanitary condition by its street-cleansing and refuse-removal services, and by its sewerage system, and its several plants for sewage disposal, refuse-destruction, and the recovery of salvage.

'Services such as these last mentioned are obviously the basic and indispensable ones for civilised life in any modern urban community; but the Local Authority does not stop short at communal provision of this kind but is an agent of mental and aesthetic culture. In almost any city or large town in England our citizen may find his tastes and interests catered for by a municipal art gallery, museum, and reference library; and lending libraries will be available for him whether he lives in town or country. When he goes on holiday to the seaside he finds the muncipality catering for his lighter amusement in forms too innumerable to describe. Finally, as the average citizen enters his declining years, illness and want may call once more for the Local Authority's succour through its Public Assistance and Medical Services; and whether this be so or not, and whether he die young or old, he will, more likely than not, be interred in the municipal cemetery, or cremated in a municipal crematorium.'[1]

This account needs some modification to-day. The Local Authority hospitals have passed over to the agencies of the new National Health Service, i.e. the Regional Hospital Boards and the Hospital Management Committees. The Poor Law has been finally 'broken up' on the lines advocated by the Webbs in their famous Minority Report of the Poor Law Commission of 1909; though certain functions such as the care of aged and infirm people in residential institutions, of various classes of disabled persons such as the blind, the deaf, and the dumb, and of children lacking proper parental care, some of which were developed as Poor Law functions, remain with the Local Authorities to be integrated in a new service and developed on new and better lines. The provision of electricity and gas is undertaken now by national agencies in place of those municipalities or privately owned 'utility companies' which were the 'undertakers' before the nationalization measures of 1946 (the Electricity Act) and 1948 (the Gas Industry Act). Under the Transport Act of 1947 it is possible that in some areas new agencies will replace the Local Authorities in the provision of street passenger transport. Water undertakings are mostly owned and managed still by Local Authorities, but there is talk of 'nationalizing'

[1] *The English Local Government System.*

this service too. The loss of functions has been heavy and is hardly compensated by some additional powers given in post-war legislation for the carrying on of 'British Restaurants' and for enabling Local Authorities to give limited financial assistance to cultural activities. But the impacts of Local Authority activity on the daily life of the citizen are still many and varied.

Such a position has been reached by piecemeal and cumulative expansion since the beginnings of the nineteenth century. It is not to be expected, therefore, that the Local Authority services which touch the citizen in the ways recited are capable of neat classification. The development and expansion of modern Local Government functions reflects the whole play of economic social and political forces since the Industrial Revolution. The aims and motives which have led to the establishment of the services differ considerably from service to service and have led to differing policies and parliamentary prescriptions for their conduct. Some services have been initiated in the locality through Private Bill legislation promoted by the local Authority, and in many cases still rest on parliamentary powers of this kind. Others rest on general statutes which have long ago replaced local legislation as the codes governing their conduct. Yet others are in the hands of the Local Authorities because the Local Authorities have been brought in politically, if not legally, as agents of the State for measures of social reform or improvement; measures which have been fashioned by the Central Government, but left to the Local Authorities for local application. Some services remain entirely at local charge while others are heavily subsidised by the Exchequer. Some services are largely free of central administrative control and others are very much subject to it.

We can, however, distinguish four groups, with some characteristic features.

Spheres of Normal Activity

The first embraces 'Protective Services', of which the Police and Fire Protection Services are the most notable. Also included in this class, however, is the wide miscellany of regulative and inspectoral work involved in sanitation, building regulation, the control of food supply, the checking of weights and measures, and similar regulative functions. Perhaps Town and Country Planning is also to be included in this category if we think of its restrictive aspects. It has, of course, a very positive value in promoting welfare, amenity, and comfort. That is also true, in fact, of many of the services in this category. Some of these services, such as the Police and Fire Services, attract Government grant in various forms, but for the most part they are sustained at the charge of the rates.

In the second group fall services such as sewering, sewage disposal, public cleansing, public lighting, and the provision and maintenance of streets and roads (except the trunk roads, for which the Ministry of Transport is responsible but which certain Local Authorities maintain as agents of the Ministry). These we may call the 'Communal Services', because all need them, all are served by them, and, on the whole, all use them as needed and pay for them collectively through rates or taxes. Specific Exchequer grants are available in one or two instances, e.g. for road improvements and rural sewage schemes; but while the diffused benefit of the Exchequer block grant must not be overlooked, the majority of services in this group are largely kept on foot by local rates. This situation is partly to be explained on historical grounds, since most of the services originated in local initiative to cope with conditions in the industrial towns. Correspondingly, since these services have been built up by local action the Local Authorities have retained a fairly wide freedom from central control in their administration.

The third group of services may be called 'Social Services' and it comprises Education and its associated medical services, Housing, Maternity and Child Welfare, and certain 'welfare' services for the aged, children, and classes needing special care. In services like these, large sections of the public are served considerably below cost; others not at all, or but slightly. The total cost is borne partly by the State out of national tax-revenue and partly out of local rates. National taxes are largely levied according to ability to pay, without regard to the individual service which the State may render; and in respect of the services under consideration this is broadly true of the local rates. The poorer sections of the community are thus helped by the richer and provided with services they could not otherwise afford. The central subventions are given in a variety of ways, but are very substantial in the aggregate.

The fourth group is that of the 'Trading Services', comprising 'public utility' services, which until recently included the supply of electricity and gas, but are now largely confined to the provision of water and street transport. Some Local Authorities run special enterprises, such as docks, tunnels, and bridges; and Hull still retains its own local telephone service. The trading services usually involve operations of an industrial character. They are maintained on a self-supporting basis without charge to the rates. They were capitalized, not out of the rates, but by borrowings on the security of the rate revenues and the Local Authority's rating powers, and the rates thus constituted 'collateral security' of a kind which usually ensured a supply of capital at very economic rates. The service is charged for on the commercial principle, i.e. the charge is related to individual use or service. The trading undertakings often make a revenue surplus, or a net profit, which, if not applied in reduction of prices, is credited to a common good fund, available for the provision of general municipal amenities, or applied, within limits, in relief of local rates.

Achievements in National Emergency

Our review so far has extended solely to the Local Authorities' normal peacetime functions and would be incomplete if it did not make some reference to all that the Local Authorities have been called upon to do in conditions of emergency, such as industrial strife, extensive flood, and, above all, the maintenance of the civil front and the succour of the community in time of war. Their outstanding achievement in this sphere was the organization and maintenance of the Civil Defence, Air Raid Precautions, and Fire Protection Services during the war of 1939–45. When the history of modern Local Government is written, the record of these activities will be one of its most impressive chapters. The responsibilities which the Local Authorities assumed were of extraordinary range and magnitude. They arranged for the evacuation from cities and towns of mothers and children, the aged and infirm, and for billeting them in 'reception areas'. To every household they distributed some form of domestic air-raid shelter, and made extensive provision for the shelter of the public in its daily goings and comings in all places of public resort and in the busy streets of our towns. The Air Raid Precautions and Fire Protection Services in a variety of forms entailed the levy and training of almost the entire male civilian population, as well as many specialist corps, for service in the Fire Guard, the Wardens Service, the Rescue Squads, the Decontamination Squads, the First Aid and Ambulance Corps, or in the Control Rooms, i.e. the nerve centres of control and communication which deployed the services to meet the particular kind and scale of enemy attack.

In some areas the Local Authorities were called upon to establish and maintain elaborate layouts of smoke-producing oil lamps to provide smoke screens for vital objectives.

After the fall of France, and in face of the threat of imminent invasion, the Local Authorities in the coastal and southerly regions of the country were called upon to establish Invasion Defence Committees, and these bodies and the Local Authority's officers co-operated with the military authorities in devising local defence plans, and were exercised in the co-ordination of measures for assisting the military authorities and handling the civilian population.

Nor did the task of the Local Authorities in dealing with enemy air attacks or the threat of invasion exhaust their war-time responsibilities. They were called upon to increase the production of food by a tremendous development of their functions as authorities under the Allotments and Small Holdings Acts, and were given large powers to bring uncultivated land into production, either by arrangement with farmers or others who could undertake the direct work of cultivation, or, if necessary, by becoming cultivators themselves. They were given large powers to deal with the wartime movements of population, not only by housing refugees, but by housing workers who had to be transferred from one area to another to meet the needs of wartime armament production. In some areas, indeed, the Local Authorities or their officers were given complete control of all vacant accommodation in the area, so that these objects might be achieved. They established communal feeding centres, so that the working population, moving from place to place, might find all necessary facilities for feeding, and the difficulties of the rationing system be eased in its bearing upon the mobile elements of the civil population. The Local Authorities were not made directly responsible for national registration or the rationing of food and fuel. But they were responsible for setting up the local committees to organize this work under the control of the responsible ministries, and throughout the major part of the war their officers, mostly Town Clerks or Borough Treasurers, undertook the local organization and control in these matters for the Central Authorities.

It needs to be appreciated that, colossal though the range of these new responsibilities was, Local Authorities and their officers had to assume them while, at the same time, continuing most of their normal peacetime functions. This situation is itself a further testimony to the vital character of Local Authorities' normal services. Naturally in conditions of war there were some functions of the Local Authorities, relating purely to amenities, which could be, and were, held in suspense. By and large, however, it is true to say that the Local Authorities' normal services had to be carried in war no less than in peace, though in vastly more difficult conditions.

The situation we have just described is perhaps the most striking proof that could be afforded of the virtues of maintaining an efficient standing system of Local Government. The planning of these new services unquestionably owed much to the Central Authorities, which had indeed necessarily to assume the responsibility for this part of the task, since they, and they alone, had the knowledge derived from the Defence Services of the kinds of situation to be met.

But it is inconceivable that services of this kind could have been centrally carried on. When central planning was pushed to its furthest point, the work of organization, and certainly the enlistment of citizen aid, had necessarily to be left to the Local Authorities. And the situation was such that local improvisation was absolutely indispensable. There were, of course, difficulties. The Local Government system had not been primarily designed as an administrative framework for the handling of tasks of so novel a kind. The area-system of Local Government, already under strain in regard to normal peacetime functions, created many difficulties in the organization of Civil Defence services, particularly in the county areas in which responsibility is divided amongst several authorities. It was necessary to fit the various Local Authorities operating in a county, for example, into a variety of *ad hoc* arrangements for divided but co-ordinated responsibility; and even in areas such as the large cities it was necessary for independent authorities, such as the County Borough Councils, to work in conjunction with adjoining authorities beyond their boundaries. Some of these difficulties admittedly became acute, but by super-human effort they were overcome, and on the whole it can be said that the Local Authorities surmounted their tasks with very great credit. The situation was one which showed that, despite defects in structure, the system of Local Authority administration itself is a resilient one capable of absorbing entirely new and novel tasks, and, what is most important of all, of enlisting the active support of the community in so doing.

Financial Yardsticks

A rough idea of the magnitude of Local Authority responsibilities in financial terms can be gathered from a few figures relating to Local Authority expenditure.

For the year 1947–8 the aggregate expenditure was £960 million. The corresponding figure representing revenue from all sources was £957,000,000, and of this, £283,000,000 was raised from rates, £269,000,000 was the total of Exchequer grants, and the balance represented revenue from trading undertakings and property, and other miscellaneous sources. The gross outstanding loan debt of the Local Authorities in this same year was £1,713,000,000, this figure representing, broadly speaking, the Local Authorities' capital. This figure does not represent, however, the total capital raised by the Local Authorities over their whole history, as Local Authorities are subject to a system of amortization of their borrowings for capital purposes by a process of annual redemption of capital debt.

So matters stood in the year before the Local Authorities' hospital, gas and electricity undertakings were transferred to the new national agencies.

Another significant year is 1913–14, representing the close of the peaceful century. In this year the total expenditure on revenue account was £148,000,000; and, of this, expenditure on trading and other remunerative properties amounted to £44,500,000; and of the balance of £93,500,000, £71,000,000 was defrayed from rate revenue, and about £22,500,000 from Exchequer grant. The gross outstanding debt was £562,000,000. In the same year, the ordinary expenditure provided for in the nation's budget was £179,000,000. It will be seen that the Local Authorities' aggregate expenditure was only some £20,000,000 less than that of the State. When it is remembered that the defence services accounted for much of the budgetary figure, it is manifest that the bulk of public expenditure for Civil Government and services, in the period before the First World War, was Local Authority expenditure. In the years which followed, between the two wars, the Local Authorities were to develop the social services, with increasing charge to their own revenues, and increased aid from the State; but the proportion of their expenditure to civil State expenditure diminished, as some new social services were established under State agencies, and, later on, these took over some of the Local Authorities' social services.

Comparisons with Other Countries

As matters stood in 1939 the scope of British Local Government was the widest in the world. Nowhere else could one find Local Government entrusted with a complex of responsibilities such as that entailed in the four spheres— each in turn so varied—of protective, communal, trading, and social services. Many services included in the first two spheres were, and still are, characteristic of Local Government in most developed countries; though even here the responsibility of British Local Authorities for Police Forces is, practically speaking, a unique one. Neither in the United States nor the major countries of Europe did the Local Authorities handle four trading services such as the provision of gas, water, electricity, and street transport to the extent that British Local Authorities did. In America such under- takings remained mostly in the hands of 'public utility companies'; and while this was so to a less extent in many European countries, the responsibility of the Local Authori- ties there was often confined to financial participation in a 'mixed undertaking'. In the sphere of the social services, the responsibilities of British Local Authorities in the system of public education are almost as unique an arrangement as their responsibilities in the maintenance of Police Forces; and the welfare services developed by British Local Authori- ties between the two wars, extending to the inauguration of the clinical health services, an enormous expansion of hous- ing provision, and the reorientation of the Poor Law, were far wider in their scope than anything undertaken in America, and were equalled, perhaps, only in the countries of Scandinavia.

The loss of functions since 1939 has been heavy, but, coming as it did chiefly in the trading sphere, and to a less extent in the social services, it is still doubtful whether the scope of British Local Government is yet surpassed, much as it may have lost its old lead in this respect.

Britain, too, has been the pioneer in most of the modern functions of Local Government. As the first country to be industrialized in the modern sense of the term, this in some ways was only to be expected. But despite all that has been said by social historians about our tardy response to the impact of the industrial revolution, it remains true that, when the response did come, it came chiefly through the agencies of Local Government, and Professor Halévy avers that it was not always so tardy as has been thought. Even the turnpike roads were the best in Europe, if we accept the testimony of a contemporary French civil engineer of high repute. Professor Halévy himself says that if our towns were insanitary in the early nineteenth century, the towns of Europe were more so. Some of the bodies of Improvement Commissioners which sprang up throughout the country as *ad hoc* Local Authorities had begun work of this kind at the beginning of the nineteenth century. Well before the end of the century English sanitation was world-famous, and its methods and equipment were being copied everywhere. One or two bodies of Commissioners had begun the municipal supply of water or gas even before 1800; as, for example, the Commissioners of Manchester and Leeds. By the middle of the century most of them were buying out the company undertakers. Later, their successors were to pioneer street tramways (the first in Europe being laid in Birkenhead in 1860); and from 1880 onwards municipalities all over the country were pioneering the electricity supply industry. In public, technical, and secondary education we lagged behind Germany in the latter part of the century, but, on the other hand, we pioneered the Public Library.

This mounting achievement was predominantly the result of local initiative. The bodies of Improvement Commissioners responsible for the earlier phases of it originated, indeed, as voluntary associations of local inhabitants, and in many instances worked for a long period without statutory powers. The trading services were inaugurated by Local Authorities almost entirely in the teeth of parliamentary opposition. If social services like school feeding, maternity and child welfare, and others of the personal health services, now form part of what are in effect national services run locally, there was a period between 1906 and the close of the First World War when what was done was largely the result of municipal experiment.

The Officer's Rôle

What is the part of the Local Government officer in all the activities and responsibilities we have now sketched? A full answer cannot be given at this stage. It is, in fact, one of the objects of the whole book to furnish such an answer, and it must be based, in any event, upon an understanding of the relation of the Local Government officer to his employing Council and to the public, which we deal with specially in Chapter V. Something can, however, be said in a preliminary way.

The main rôle of the Service and the individual officer is to carry into execution duties for which the Local Authority is responsible, and policies which it devises within the limits of its local discretion. Even in the sphere of executive action, it is obvious that much will depend on the skill, the training, the qualifications, the probity, the tact, and the zeal of the Local Government officers engaged. It is manifest, too, that over so wide and varied a range of functions, the experience and knowledge of Local Government officers must be similarly varied and wide. The requirements are exacting enough if one particular service is considered, but it is evident that those officers who are concerned with administration, finance, or works ranging over the whole extent of the Local Authorities' functions, such as the Clerk, the Treasurer and the Engineer, have responsibilities of a still higher order; the Clerk in particular, since he is concerned with the administrative efficiency of the whole framework and mechanism in a 'complex' of varied services.

Chief officers are expected, however, to tender their advice on many questions of policy. By the very continuity of their responsibilities, apart altogether from any other circumstance, they can form an all-round consciousness of local community need, which makes their advice particularly valuable in essaying the provision to be made (present or future) for a given community. The responsibilities of these officers really go beyond, therefore, the executive and managerial functions that are their primary responsibility.

Nor is the Local Authority the only party which seeks

their advice. The Local Authorities are organized into associations which consider the general interests of Local Authorities and the impact of new or impending legislation. It is common practice for Government Departments to call these associations into consultation, and in this way many Local Government officers who become recognized as specially expert in particular fields are called upon to advise the associations and the Government Departments. This they do in a voluntary capacity.

The extent to which Local Government officers concentrate their activities upon purely administrative, executive, or managerial functions, or take the initiative in proposing policies for the consideration of their employing authorities, may vary considerably at different times, in different places, and in different services. No responsible observer can deny that there is a real place for elected representatives in the *initiation* of new measures. There have been, in successive generations, and still are, parliamentarians and prominent local citizens to whom we owe the inauguration of many new services, particularly in the epoch when the trading and the social services were developed. On the other hand, there have been eminent Local Government officers who could claim to have been the pioneers in many social experiments in the Local Government field. It is probably true to say that it was the elected representatives from whom the initiative mostly proceeded in the earlier nineteenth century. The true Local Authorities of that time were the various bodies of Town or Improvement Commissioners we have referred to, incorporated with statutory powers, but originally coming together as voluntary bodies of citizens to provide the amenities which the new towns created by the Industrial Revolution lacked. The Municipal Corporations Act of 1835 established the Boroughs on an elective basis and with a new democratic constitution, but it was a long time before the new corporations absorbed the functions of the various *ad hoc* bodies of commissioners to which resort had first been made. In these early days of improvisation and experiment, the elected representatives on these local bodies must certainly have taken the initiative in the inauguration of local services. At that epoch there was no corps of trained Local Government officers, though no doubt many practical men were found to carry out such work as sewering, paving, etc., who became paid servants of the responsible commissioners.

Conditions have been different in recent times, and while there is still a field left for the initiative of elected representatives, Local Authorities' powers in recent times have sprung much more from the general social sense, as expressed in and by Parliament, than in years past. The general compass of a Local Authority's activities being now fairly well marked out, it is probably the high officers of a Local Authority who are best able to judge the long-term requirements of a particular community, such as sewage extensions, the mapping out of areas for housing, and so on, than the elected representatives who change so frequently with the results of the polls.

But once more it must be said, with emphasis, that, free as the British Local Government officer is to advise on policy and to put forward his suggestions for policy, within the Local Authority's general powers and aims, it is the members of the Local Authority in their collective and representative capacity who have the final say as to what shall, or shall not, be done, and who control the doing of it.

The wartime emergency services fell into a special category. In the nature of the case, plans had to be devised centrally for application by local staffs; though, even so, broad control and financial responsibility largely rested with their employing Councils. It is no immodest claim for the Local Government Service to say that, on the whole, the real burden of work and responsibility in the war-time services lay upon the officers, and that they can claim most of the credit for all that was done at local level in organizing and deploying the citizen army for Civil Defence, in succouring the citizens in their distress, and in restoring the life of stricken towns.

CHAPTER II

Composition and Layout

As WAS stated in the introductory chapter, not all employees of our Local Authorities are 'officers'. In the parlance of Local Government administration, the term 'officer' has, in fact, a special meaning and a limited denotation. It is restricted to those employees (apart altogether from teachers and police officers) whose duties are of a professional, technical, administrative, or clerical nature. This usage has been reinforced by the language of the Local Government Superannuation Act of 1937, which places superannuation arrangements for officers and manual workers on a different footing. Section 40 of the Act defines 'officers' as those employees whose duties 'are wholly or mainly administrative, professional or clerical' or 'whose remuneration is not greater than £250 per annum and whose employment is not by way of manual labour'. All other employees (apart from teachers and police officers) the Act designates as 'servants', the most numerous class among these being the manual workers.

Extent

Looked at from another standpoint, however, the term 'officer' is a very wide one. It includes such high officers as Clerks of County Councils, Town Clerks, and Clerks of District Councils; County, City, or Borough Treasurers; County, City, or Borough Engineers and Surveyors; Medical Officers of Health; Chief Education Officers; County, City, or Borough Architects; and other administrative, professional, or managerial officers whose status is that of chief officers. It includes the varied classes of professional, technical, or administrative officers who are their deputies, or their principal or senior assistants. It also includes, however, not only the senior grades of subordinate officers, but the rank and file of the numerous class of clerical employees, not omitting shorthand-typists and office-machine operators.

It is probably true that the use of the term 'officer', its extension to such employees as clerks, on the one hand, and its exclusion of manual workers, however skilled and well paid, on the other, owes something to past notions of the social prestige of various occupations. But, as the humbler classes of clerk in the Local Government Service are acutely realising, recent changes in social and economic conditions have considerably impaired the distinctions between themselves and the manual workers. A recent enquiry conducted by the London School of Economics into the social prestige accorded to particular occupations affords ample evidence, if any were needed, of the fact that a routine clerk is no longer counted higher in the scale of social prestige than the skilled manual worker. Nor are the overall differences in the total remuneration of clerks and manual workers, respectively, what they were.

There are still, however, important differences of status between the officers, even those at the lowest levels, and the manual workers; though these, apart from the differentiation for superannuation purposes, rest much less than is commonly supposed upon legal prescriptions, and arise chiefly from the different kinds of contract of service which Local Authorities, following the practice of employers generally, apply to the two broad classes of employee.

The officers are usually remunerated by a salary, expressed in yearly terms and paid monthly, whereas the manual workers are paid by weekly, or, in some cases, daily or hourly, wages. The officers enjoy an entitlement to holidays and certain guaranteed rights as to sick pay which on the whole are better than those of the manual workers. As against this, the manual workers receive payment for overtime, whereas the officers at higher levels do not; and although payment for overtime has been introduced for officers at the lower levels, the conditions and rates of payment are not comparable with, or, in fact, as good as, those enjoyed by the manual workers. The officers have usually the right to a month's, and sometimes a quarter's, notice, whereas the manual workers have, generally speaking, the right to no more than a week's notice.

Subject to any rights to notice, however, the officers enjoy in law no greater security of tenure than the manual workers, save in exceptional cases which will be discussed later on. The popular impression that the officers legally hold office for life, or until retirement, is quite erroneous. With the exceptions referred to, they hold their office 'at the pleasure of the Council', subject to any contractual conditions as to notice. Officers are not usually dismissed except for good cause. Nor indeed are manual workers; and while the Local Authority has a discretion as to the manual workers it will bring within the statutory scheme for superannuation, the majority are included, and enjoy in practice a security of tenure not less than that of the officers, and participate in superannuation benefits at less charge to themselves.

When, however, an office is abolished by statute (and only then) it is legislative practice to provide for the payment of 'compensation for loss of office'. This practice is based upon a recognition of the circumstances in which officers normally take up office in the public service. They do so in normal expectation of a continuous career. They submit themselves as public servants to many restrictions not operative in the commercial and industrial world. They expect a livelihood which has some relation to their qualifications and responsibilities as they progress in the Service; but they know beforehand that they can never win the glittering prizes of the commercial or industrial world, or, however brilliant they may be if they are professional men, reach the high levels of remuneration of the most successful private practitioner. The burden of compensation on the public purse has, however, not been a heavy one at any time. The amount of compensation is governed by a scale related to years of service and the remuneration reached, and can seldom be higher than corresponding pension rates. Quite apart from this, however, loss of office usually occurs when one public service is being merged into another, and the bulk of the staffs are transferred. Compensation is then not payable, or only payable in respect of any diminution of emoluments.

It is unnecessary for the purposes of this book to enter into the merits or justification of these differences between officers and manual workers. They are described in the broadest possible terms, are not exhaustive, and are meant only as illustrations of the main differences which distinguish the employees dealt with in this book from the manual workers. They will help us to understand one further difference between the two classes; i.e. that they are dealt with separately in the practice and procedure of Local Authorities in the management of their personnel, and by different machinery for negotiation and collective bargaining. Irrespective of any question as to levels of remuneration, it is in the nature of things that classes of employee whose duties are so dissimilar should be separately dealt with. It is impossible to measure the output of the two classes in the same way. Yardsticks of measurement which are available in the case of the manual worker are simply not available in the case of the clerk, and still less for the officers at a higher level than a clerk. An appreciation of such differing circumstances as these is material in appreciating many of the service conditions which we shall be discussing.

It is to be hoped that the term 'officer' will never be abandoned in favour of one which sometimes comes into popular use, namely, 'official'. This latter term carries, and is sometimes meant to carry when used in quarters which regard all public servants as enemies of the people, something of the sense of 'officious'. It is no part of the ideals of the Local Government officer to be officious, nor do the vast majority of Local Government officers prove to be so. In any event, both on the constitutional and on the human plane, their relationship with the public and with their employers is of a kind which effectively precludes the development of any spirit of this kind. They are in fact as much 'servants' as the manual workers and would be the first to acknowledge themselves as such.

The numerical strength of the Service is a matter of some conjecture. Neither past nor current statistics of the Ministry of Labour, or Census data, furnish any authentic figure for the officer class in Local Authority employ. The National Joint Council for Local Authorities' Administrative, Professional, Technical and Clerical Staffs (England and Wales), a body to which we shall be making frequent reference, has recently estimated that the number of officers in England and Wales covered by its Scheme of Conditions of Service (excluding those employed only on a temporary basis) was 150,000 as at 31st October 1948. It is not clear whether the estimate includes the staffs of the London County Council and the Corporation of the City of London —which have remained outside the National Joint Council and its Scheme. The estimate (contained in a document entitled *A Survey of the Local Service* and published in 1950, setting out information as to the implementation of the National Joint Council's Scheme of Conditions of Service) is based upon questionnaires issued by the Council when electricity and gas staffs were in transition from Local Authority employ to the employ of the new Authorities under the post-war nationalization measures in these spheres. On these and other grounds the estimate must be regarded with some reserve. No official estimate of a similar character has been made by the separate but similar body which functions for Scotland, but its secretariat regards the number of officers in Scotland as about 13,000 or 14,000.

Occupational Range

The occupational range of the Service is extremely varied. In the first edition of *The English Local Government System*, published in 1946, the author gave the following catalogue of Local Government occupations:

'All aspects of the municipality's work call for the services of administrators, lawyers, accountants, architects, civil engineers, surveyors, and valuers. The public health and medical services employ physicians, surgeons, dentists, orthopaedists, bacteriologists, alienists, psychologists, psychiatrists, radiologists, pharmaceutical chemists, analysts, dispensers, opticians, almoners, dietitians, chaplains, cemetery and mortuary superintendents, and every kind of nursing staff. The sanitary services, such as sewerage and water supply, employ engineers, industrial chemists, and agriculturalists. The education services employ every kind of school-teacher, primary, secondary, technical, scientific and classical, not to speak of instructors in art, music, and handicrafts, and teachers in physical training. The various "protective" services employ police officers, coroners, fire brigade officers, sanitary inspectors, weights and measures inspectors, veterinary officers, etc. The public utility services employ gas engineers, water engineers, electrical engineers, transport managers, and in some places aerodrome managers, tunnel managers, bridge managers, harbour and dock managers and ferries managers (with various grades of ships' officers and engineers). The cultural activities engage the services of librarians, curators of museums, curators of art galleries (with staffs of scientists and experts in applied art), organists, orchestral conductors, musicians and bandsmen. The recreational services employ horticulturists, landscape-gardeners, professional golfers, golf-course managers, and swimming instructors. Nor are there wanting one or two odd professions and occupations such as rat-catchers, water-diviners, oyster-bed cultivators, and race-course managers.'

In addition, there are, of course, the clerks, typists, and office machine-operators, who form the basic grades of the non-manual staffs.

Owing to the transfers to nationalized services which we have mentioned, gas and electrical engineers must now come out of the list. Some of the technicians in the health service must come out, too; though not all, because some still remain attached to Local Government health services. The aerodrome managers may still be left in, though they are a very small class, most of the municipal aerodromes having been taken over by the Ministry of Civil Aviation. The same is true of valuers, most of whom were engaged in valuation for rating, a function since transferred to the Board of Inland Revenue. It may be doubted whether any recent additions to Local Authorities' powers, which by no means compensate in scale for those they have lost, entail any appreciable additions to the catalogue. Restaurant managers might perhaps be added, Local Authorities having now been empowered to continue on certain conditions the 'British restaurants' which they managed during the war. Although Local Authorities have also been given certain powers to give financial assistance to cultural amenities it may be doubted whether the municipal jester and the local municipal music-hall artist will appear in the list just yet.

All these occupational groups the National Joint Council's 'Scheme of Conditions of Service' classifies up to a salary level of £1,000 a year (beyond which other machinery operates) into the following divisions: a General Division, a Clerical Division, a Higher Clerical Division, and an Administrative, Professional and Technical Division. In addition, a supplementary scheme of the Council's provides a Miscellaneous Division for officers at a lower level whose duties are not entirely clerical. According to the Council's *Survey*, already referred to, 42.8 per cent of the staffs were in the General Division, 7.9 per cent in the Miscellaneous Division (since, however, extended, with many consequent shifts of classification as between this division and others); about 12.2 per cent were in the Clerical and Higher Clerical Divisions; and of the remainder 35 per cent were in the Administrative, Professional and Technical Divisions up to the limit of the Council's jurisdiction at £1,000 a year; leaving 2.2 per cent at levels over £1,000 a year. About 30 per cent of the total staff were women, and 79 per cent of them were in the General Division.

The A.P.T. Division comprises a skeleton framework of ten scales into which various posts can be 'slotted' for grading purposes. There is no automatic progression from one to another of the ten scales. The lowest of them begins just above the maximum of the General Division. It is therefore evident that the administrative section of this division of the Local Government Service is something different in character, composition and status from the administrative class of the Civil Service. The class in the Local Government Service which is nearest in status and function is comprised of the chief officers and their deputies, and a small number of their principal assistants, many of whom are above the National Joint Council's 'ceiling'. They are, however, distinguished from their Civil Service prototypes in having had, for the most part, a professional training. We shall discuss these differences later on.

Distribution Under Local Government Structure

The distribution of the Local Government Service throughout the country follows the pattern of Local Government structure. The staffs are employed by the individual Local Authorities comprised in this structure. These are not of one uniform type, but of several types, each serving a particular kind of area. In order to understand how the Local Government Service is distributed throughout the country it is necessary, therefore, to describe the layout of the Local Authorities which employ them, i.e. the different types of Local Authority, their number and size, and their respective functions.

It should first be made abundantly clear that each individual Local Authority does not undertake the whole range of Local Government functions. The situation is indeed a very different one. Only in one type of area, namely, the County Borough, is the Local Authority an 'all purposes authority', i.e. one which undertakes (practically) the whole range of Local Government services. The County Borough is an urban unit which, although situate in a geographical county, is not part of the county for the purposes of Local Government. The size of these units varies. Large cities, such as Birmingham, Liverpool, Manchester and Leeds, are County Boroughs, the term 'city' having no significance in Local Government structure. The majority of the County Boroughs are, however, the medium-sized towns mostly situate in the provinces, such as Birkenhead, Blackburn, Coventry and Wolverhampton. There has been much controversy as to what should be the minimum size, in terms of population, for such units. As matters stand, the population goes down to as low a level as 50,000 or so in the case of Canterbury, but levels so low as this are exceptions, and most of the County Boroughs are, in fact, upwards of 75,000 population, though some twenty or so are just under.

Elsewhere (in England and Wales) the functions of Local Government are distributed over what may be called a 'three-tier' system. The largest unit is the administrative county. This, generally speaking, is a unit corresponding in area with the geographical county; though in certain parts of the country the geographical county has been divided into separate administrative counties. For example, Sussex is divided into East Sussex and West Sussex, and Lincoln is divided into three administrative counties, namely, Holland, Kesteven and Lindsey.

The English counties are, in turn, divided into three types of unit. The first is the non-County Borough—properly called a Municipal Borough—and representing, broadly speaking, the fairly substantial town which, though falling short of the status of the County Borough, with its independence of the administrative county and complete range of functions, has nevertheless been given the constitution of a Municipal Borough (the constitution of the County Borough being identical). Many old towns with very small populations have, however, retained the status of Municipal Boroughs. The second type of unit is the Urban District, representing the smaller town communities, or perhaps the newer ones which have not yet been promoted to the status of Borough. The third type of unit is the Rural District, representing for the most part an agricultural sub-division of the county, though it may contain urbanised pockets. One or other of these three types of unit, according to the character of particular areas, constitutes the second tier in the administrative county. The Rural District is, in turn, divided up into parishes; so that in Rural Districts, but not elsewhere, we get a third tier. The less populous of the parishes have their affairs looked after by a primary assembly of the inhabitants called a Parish Meeting, but the more populous of them have a Parish Council.

The distribution of functions outside the County Boroughs to the authorities at the three levels within the administrative county follows a pattern of great intricacy and, as most people would say, little logicality. There have been many reshuffles in recent years, including a considerable number since 1945. In the following paragraph we give only a very broad account of the position; and for detail the reader must be referred to works on the Local Government System as such. The merits of the situation are a matter of controversy.

The County Councils take the large-scale services and those in which it has been the policy to spread the charge over the ratepayers of the county rather than those of smaller areas within it. We find, therefore, the County Council undertaking the Police, Fire, and Ambulance Services; the Education Service (including the school medical service); the upkeep, improvement and maintenance of county roads (though here there are intricate arrangements for the Boroughs, Urban Districts and Rural Districts to undertake in varying measure certain functions in their own areas as agents for the County Council); the Maternity and Child Welfare and the Clinical Health Services; the care of children lacking parental care, aged persons, and others requiring special care, such as the blind, deaf and dumb; and in certain areas some of the regulative services such as the inspection of weights and measures, and the enforcement of shop regulations.

On the other hand, the Boroughs, Urban Districts and Rural Districts undertake the local communal services, and particularly those relating to sanitation and building development, though the wider aspects of Town and Country Planning are in the hands of the County. In the case of the Boroughs and Urban Districts, the aggregate of these services is very considerable. It is the County District Authorities, moreover (a statutory term which includes the Boroughs as well as the Urban Districts and Rural Districts) which undertake the important service of housing. The trading services are mostly undertaken by town Authorities, i.e. in the County areas, the Boroughs and Urban Districts, and few, if any, of them by the County Council; but, as we have already mentioned, the two most important of these, gas and electricity, have now been lost to Local Authority responsibility by recent measures of nationalization. It is, however, still the town authorities (including the County Boroughs, the Boroughs and the Urban Districts), and to some extent the Rural Districts, which have the responsibility for water supply where this is in municipal hands—as it mostly is. It is these authorities, also, which undertake, although not in every area, tramway or omnibus services. Few of the personal health services now remain in the hands of the county district Authorities; but the environmental health services are amongst the most important of their functions, such as the cleansing and lighting of streets, the removal of domestic refuse, the destruction and disposal of refuse, the sewering of the locality, the disposal of sewage, the provision of parks and open spaces— and all these in addition to the administration of the regulative code for environmental public health, much of which is applied through the powers of the Local Authorities in regard to nuisances, the regulation of building, and the enforcement of standards for the maintenance of property in sanitary condition.

There is not a great deal of difference between the powers of the Borough and the Urban District, the principal difference being in respect of constitution; the Borough, like the County Borough, having a Mayor and an Aldermanic body elected by the main body of Councillors; and the Urban Districts having simply a body of Councillors, with a Chairman. Legally, perhaps, there is not as much difference between the powers of the Borough and the Urban District on the one hand, and the Rural District Council on the other hand, as is sometimes imagined; but there is, of course, an essential difference in the kind and scale of provision necessary in a sparsely populated area as distinct from that necessary in a populous and closely-built-up town. In the Rural Districts the powers of the Parish Councils or Meetings are not very wide, and relate chiefly to the upkeep of minor amenities or the enforcement of rights of way.

Scottish Local Government structure presents some differences. A status equivalent to that of the English County Boroughs is accorded only to the four large cities, i.e., Glasgow, Edinburgh, Aberdeen and Dundee, which are called 'Counties of Cities'. Elsewhere the structure is two-tier; there are no Parish Councils. The 'burghs' share functions with the County Councils; but are mostly small, with functions varying somewhat according to their size. In the 'landward', i.e. rural areas, there are District Councils comprised partly of the local County Councillors and partly of members directly elected in the locality, and these Councils carry out a few functions of their own and others delegated by the County Councils.

Having described the types of area and authority which comprise the structure of British Local Government, it is necessary to add that not only are there differences as to functions between different types of Local Authority, but there are very great disparities in the size of Local Authorities of similar type and status constitutionally. No one could expect to find completely rigid standards of size and population among Local Authorities in any one class; but the facts as they are show conclusively that, even if the present structure be retained, it requires to be completely reapplied to the changed demographic conditions which have developed in the present century. There are schools of thought which would, indeed, either change the structure radically by the creation of units of a new kind, e.g. regional, or by remoulding substantially some of the present units.

It is irrelevant to the purposes of this book to go into the reasons for the disparities we have mentioned, but it is essential to its purposes to take note of them. There are eighty-three County Boroughs, and their size ranges from Birmingham, with a population of just over a million, to Canterbury, with a population of 26,000. In England there are (in addition to the London County Council) sixty-one County Councils, ranging from Lancashire with a population of just over two million (which means 'administrative' population excluding that of the County Boroughs) down to Rutland with just over 17,000. Of Municipal Boroughs there are 309, ranging from Willesden with 179,900 to some ancient Boroughs with only a thousand or two. There are 572 Urban Districts, of which two, Harrow and Rhondda, have populations over 100,000, and a large number have populations less than 5,000. There are 475 Rural Districts ranging from 80,000 down to 5,000 or less. All figures cited represent in round numbers the Registrar-General's current estimates. There are as many as 7,000 Parish Councils and 4,100 Parish Meetings, and, while the majority of these represent little more than village populations, there are some in which the population is almost equivalent to that of many Urban District Councils and small Boroughs. There are, in addition, a number of *ad hoc* Authorities such as joint boards.

Local Government in London proper, i.e. not 'Greater London', has a structure of its own. The administrative county, i.e. the area of the London County Council, has a population of 2,600,000 or so, and the twenty-eight 'Metropolitan Boroughs' in this area range in population from Wandsworth with 332,500 to Stoke Newington with 47,649.

Differences in size and function as considerable as those we have indicated are, of course, duly reflected in the disposition of Local Authority staffs. The big employers are manifestly the County Boroughs, and next, the County Councils. Next come the Boroughs and Urban Districts, and then the Rural Districts. Few, if any, of the Parish Councils employ staff at all on a whole-time basis, though there is often a part-time Clerk.

The large County Borough is, in administrative terms, a large-scale organism of amazing scope and range. Before the transfer of gas and electricity, the City of Birmingham had an outstanding capital debt of about £65,000,000 (almost equivalent to the total capital of Unilever and Lever Bros. Ltd.). Even after transfer of these undertakings and its hospitals it administers a total annual expenditure of some £18,000,000; and has a total pay roll of about 40,000, comprising teachers, police, firemen, manual workers, and Local Government officers. The figures for Glasgow, Liverpool, and Manchester are of the same order.

The County Boroughs, and the large cities among them on an immensely greater scale, conduct all the services we have described earlier in this chapter, i.e. the vast complex of communal services, the social services, such as education and housing, the protective services, including police and fire protection; and finally, until a year ago, they were in charge mostly everywhere of four great industrial and commercial enterprises, namely, the supply and distribution of gas, electricity and water, and the provision of street transport. As part of their housing activities some of them had in effect built new towns, Manchester, for example, having created the new town of Withenshaw for a population of about 80,000. Two of the County Boroughs on the Cheshire side of the Mersey, Birkenhead and Wallasey, were distinguished by the greatest range of services of any Local Authority in the Kingdom, because they had the normal range of County Borough functions, a full quota of the four customary trading undertakings, gas, water, electricity supply and street transport; and, in addition, ran their steam ferries across the Mersey; Birkenhead, in addition, participating, with Liverpool, in the management of the unique Mersey traffic tunnel.

The London County Council has a budget of about £50,000,000, larger than that of many European states, and a total pay-roll of 60,000, of which about 9,000 represent administrative, professional, technical and clerical staffs. Owing to recent transfers of functions from Boroughs and Districts, the substantial County Councils in the provinces have in recent years taken charge of a considerable administrative 'complex' only less in scope and size than that of the large County Boroughs.

Details of the staffs employed by individual Local Authorities are tabulated in the National Joint Council's *Survey* of 1950.

The foregoing review not only throws a rather searching light upon the present condition of Local Government structure in England, a controversial theme on which, however, we do not wish to enter, but goes to show that there must be certain limits to the uniformities it is possible to introduce into the Local Government Service; and, above all, illustrates how difficult, if not impossible, it is to establish any basis for costing comparisons, in the sphere of staffing, as between one Local Authority and another.

Local Layout

Except at the extremities of size, however, administrative and other considerations set a fairly uniform pattern for departmental organization among authorities of the same type, though there are often differences in the functions of departments similarly named. A full account must be sought in works on Local Government administration, but the broad pattern is roughly as follows. In Counties, County Boroughs, and Boroughs and Districts alike, there will be separate Clerks', Finance, Engineers' and Surveyors', and Public Health Departments. The Counties and the County Boroughs will have, in addition, separate departments for police, education, and possibly public libraries. The larger cities and counties have established separate architectural departments, but elsewhere the work of such a department is assimilated in the Engineers' and Surveyors' Department. The larger Authorities often concentrate certain regulative functions in a special department, but elsewhere these may be divided among the Clerk, the Engineers and Surveyor's, and the Health Departments. For Town and Country Planning, the larger Authorities have appointed special planning officers, but the relationship of those officers' functions and that of the executive heads is dealt with on somewhat differing lines. In all types of large Authorities there may be other separate departments than those we have mentioned, e.g. for water supply, transport, markets, baths, parks, and cemeteries.

We devote the remainder of this chapter to an account of the chief officers. This will illustrate still further some of the possible variations in departmental layout.

Certain chief officers are what are called 'statutory officers', that is to say, they hold offices which Local Authorities are directed to establish by the general constitutional code for Local Government now consolidated in the Local Government Act of 1933. These, in the case of the County, County Borough, Borough, and District Councils, are the Clerk of the Council (who in the case of a County Borough or Borough is styled Town Clerk); the Treasurer (who is usually the Council's chief financial officer and accountant; the Surveyor (who is usually both engineer and surveyor); the Medical Officer of Health; and the Sanitary Inspector. All but the smaller of the Authorities mentioned usually find it necessary to appoint several sanitary inspectors, of whom one is designated Chief Sanitary Inspector.

In addition, certain Local Government statutes relating to specific services also require the appointment of a chief officer for that service. For example, police authorities must appoint a Chief Constable, and education authorities a Chief Education Officer.

The larger Local Authorities find it necessary to go beyond the range of the minimum team required by the Local Government Act of 1933 or the statutes relating to particular services. For example, until the transfer of gas and electricity undertakings to the State, those Authorities which ran such undertakings appointed a Gas Engineer and Manager and an Electrical Engineer and Manager.

Most larger Local Authorities have put their parks, baths and libraries under separate departmental Heads, while small or medium-sized Authorities may appoint specialist sectional heads for such functions but place them under the general direction of the Surveyor and Engineer, or Education Officer, respectively. Some larger Authorities create separate departments for the functions of cleansing and lighting; others appoint separate cleansing superintendents or lighting superintendents, with responsibility to the Engineer and Surveyor. Again, while in small- or medium-sized Authorities we find the Engineer and Surveyor acting also as the Council's Architect, in larger cities and counties a City or County Architect may be appointed. It is not often, however, that the functions of Engineer and Surveyor are separated, though this is the case in Manchester, where there are separate departments under a City Surveyor, City Engineer, and a City Architect. The extent to which functions are integrated or divided depends largely, of course, on the size of the Authority, the volume of work, and other administrative considerations into which we need not enter here.

The relations which obtain between chief officers for the purpose of the Council's work belong to a study of the Local Government System in its administrative aspects which must be pursued elsewhere (see, for example, the author's *Municipal Administration*).

Chief Officers

As to their relative status, it is only possible to give the broadest indications, in view of the differences in local conditions to which reference has been made. The Clerk of the Council, or Town Clerk, is regarded practically everywhere as the Principal Officer of the Council. Below the level of the Clerk, the relative status of the other chief officers varies considerably from place to place, not always following the type, or even the size, of Authorities. And at this next level relative status may in some respects rest on nothing more than differences in remuneration arising from the particular assessment which the individual Authority may make of the responsibilities of the several offices, and 'the rate for the job' in each case. The Treasurer, the Engineer and Surveyor, and the Medical Officer, and, if the Authority has an Education Authority, the Chief Education Officer, are often remunerated at much the same level. In some places the Borough Engineer and Surveyor is looked upon as the officer next in status to the Town Clerk; and in others the Chief Financial Officer.

Local Government legislation requires, as we have said, the appointment of certain chief officers, as already listed, but says very little indeed about the functions they are to perform, a situation which is understandable perhaps in the light of the differing conditions we have described. While, therefore, an indication of the functions of 'the statutory officers' is useful at this stage, it can only be given in the broadest terms.

Even the responsibilities of the office of Town Clerk may vary considerably from place to place. At a minimum, the duties are those of a Secretary to the Council and to its Committees, and of the Council's principal correspondent and agent of communication with the citizens and all with whom the Council has to deal. Other chief officers and departmental heads may conduct their specialized correspondence, but in all matters of policy and general concern the Town Clerk is the Local Authority's mouthpiece. It has been found convenient and advantageous in Local Government, as in other spheres, that the Secretary of the governing body should also be its Legal Officer. Hence most Clerks of Councils and Town Clerks fulfil the dual rôle. The statutes do not require the Clerk to be a lawyer. In practice, Local Authorities usually require a professional legal qualification,

D

and usually prefer the qualification of Solicitor to that of Barrister. The Local Authority's legal work is, of course, very extensive. Working in the discharge of its responsibilities within a framework of legislation, as it must do, and being also amenable to the general rules of law in most of its relationships with third parties, the Local Authority finds need for legal advice at every stage. Moreover, much of its work must be carried out by contract and is dependent upon the acquisition of land. The Town Clerk is usually responsible for all contracts and conveyancing and for much of the preparatory negotiation. He institutes proceedings in court for the enforcement of local by-laws, regulative statutory codes, and civil litigation for the defence of the Council's interests. But the growth of Local Government responsibilities and the corresponding development of the Council's administrative and executive machinery have called upon the Town Clerk to be something more than Secretary or Legal Officer. To an increasing extent he has been given a general oversight of the Council's administrative mechanisms. Many authorities in recent years have reinforced his position by styling him Chief Administrative and Executive Officer. As a matter of fact, agreement has recently been reached between representatives of Town Clerks and of Local Authorities for the Town Clerk to be styled 'Chief Administrative and Executive Officer'. There are many incidental duties attached to the office which defy classification. For instance, the Clerk runs the local elections, and is usually resorted to for the preparation of the electoral register, and the conduct of elections for Parliament. Finally, he is called upon to advise the Mayor not only on matters connected with the Mayor's discharge of his functions as Chairman of the Council, but in many of the customary and traditional duties which English mayors discharge. Arrangements for ceremonial, hospitality, and public observances, whether under the auspices of the Council as such, or under the auspices of the Mayor, are a still further range of duties which customarily descend on the Town Clerk's shoulders.

The Council's Chief Financial Officer may or may not be appointed Treasurer within the meaning of the Local

Government statutes, but he customarily is so designated except in very small Authorities. He acts as the Council's collector of revenues, its paymaster, its accountant, and advisor on all financial aspects of the Council's functions. We have already given some figures as to the measure of the Local Authority's financial responsibilities, and it must be manifest without further specification how onerous the Chief Financial Officer's duties must be.

The duties of the Engineer and Surveyor vary somewhat according to the type of authority, but are everywhere of an extremely varied and responsible character. The making or maintenance of highways and bridges, the regulation of building development, sewage and drainage, sewage disposal, are everywhere a staple element in the responsibilities. Except in the largest cities, the duties may extend to housing, the provision and maintenance of public buildings, refuse collection and disposal, street lighting, and all works and maintenance connected with the layout or maintenance of parks, recreation grounds, public spaces, and so on. In small- or medium-sized Authorities the Engineer and Surveyor may also be Water Engineer. Everywhere he has a concern with Town and Country Planning in some of its most fundamental aspects.

The Medical Officer of Health, no matter what Authority he serves, exercises a general watch over the health of the community. He has special responsibilities for guarding against or dealing with infectious disease, and must maintain a close watch over the general sanitary conditions of the area. Recent transfers of health functions to the new National Health services, and reshuffles of responsibility from Borough and District to County Council in the sphere of health services which remain under Local Authority charge, have in recent years brought about many changes in the levels of responsibility of Medical Officers serving the various types and sizes of authority. The responsibilities of the County Medical Officers have increased. Apart from the general duties already mentioned, they control such clinical services as Maternity and Child Welfare, and the School Medical Services. The Borough and District Medical Officers have lost some responsibilities in direction, but are still continuing professional work of a clinical nature, their services being utilized, in the Borough and District areas, in the discharge of the County Council's responsibilities in this type of work, under arrangements made between the County Councils and the Borough and District Councils.

The Sanitary Inspector is an officer whose duties, exceptionally, have been prescribed in some detail by statutory orders. The inspectors work under the general direction of the Medical Officer of Health, but in some respects the law speaks directly to them and they have a sphere of direct responsibility. Their work is a miscellany of wide range, including vital functions in the suppression of nuisances, maintenance of sanitation, enforcement of proper standards in the purity of food, milk, and drugs, and proper standards of cleanliness in the sale of meat and other commodities.

CHAPTER III

Development as a Service

TOWN CLERKS have made the pleasing discovery, for purposes of post-prandial discourse, that the antiquity of their office is attested by Holy Writ. In the nineteenth chapter of the Acts of the Apostles we may indeed read of the successful intervention of the Town Clerk of Ephesus in the unruly scenes provoked by Demetrius, the silversmith, on the entry of Paul and his companions into that city. 'The Town Clerk appeased the people' with a speech of such characteristic wisdom that the apostle reports it in full. Moreover, 'when he had thus spoken he dismissed the assembly' in an open display of power which our 'grey eminences' of to-day might think a little risky.

Probably no Town Clerk has taken the passage as testifying to the existence of any office similar to his own during the Roman suzerainty. It is, however, unmistakable evidence that the office of Town Clerk was one very familiar to the public in the age of the Authorized Version of the English Bible. From other sources it could be shown that the office of Town Clerk goes back even farther. Some of our ancient cities preserve complete rolls of their Mayors and Town Clerks since the Middle Ages; and in all likelihood some such office as that of Town Clerk existed under the very earliest charters granted to the ancient municipal corporations. The Municipal Corporations Act of 1835, which swept the ancient corporations away, and introduced the new model we know to-day, preserved some of the old municipal offices, including that of Town Clerk; and in this office, therefore, and in one or two others such as that of Comptroller or Chamberlain—titles still preserved by some City or Borough Treasurers—we have a continuous link between the Local Government officer of to-day and the Local Government officer of the remote past.

Origins

To trace the remote lineage of the Service through such ancient offices would doubtless provide much lore of human interest to the Local Government officer and much material of value to the student of social history; but the practical aim we have set before us in this book precludes such a study. Both our Local Government System and the Local Government Service have links with the past, but for the most part they are the products of the Industrial Revolution, and we can go no farther back than this.

In the modern epoch, paid Local Government officers make their first appearance as employees of the *ad hoc* bodies of Town Commissioners which we referred to in the opening chapter and which were variously named Improvement, Lighting, Paving, or Watching Commissioners. Not until some decades after 1835 would most of these officers pass into the service of the municipal corporations established under the Act of 1835. The *ad hoc* Highway Boards established under the Highways Act of 1835, and the Boards of Health established under the Public Health Act of 1848, would also have paid officers, until their functions also were absorbed by the municipal corporations, or by the Urban and Rural District Councils established under the legislation of 1894. The County Councils established in 1888 would take over paid officers who had hitherto served the Justices of the Peace in Quarter Sessions in the discharge of those administrative functions which Quarter Sessions continued to carry out in rural areas until the advent of the County Councils.

After 1894 there must have been a considerable number of Local Government officers in the service of the Local Authorities we know to-day. The functions of these Local Authorities ranged over the protective, the communal, and the trading services, and must already have represented a fair proportion of the occupational range of the Service to-day.

But not even at the turn of the century could this body of paid servants be described collectively as a Service. And in tracing the events which have stamped a congeries of locally appointed officers with the character of a Service, we can begin no earlier than the years before the First World War; and shall find the process not very far advanced until the years before the Second World War, and not quite complete until after its close.

Sense of the Term 'Service'

But before we trace the history of these years we must dispose of a fundamental question. What do we mean by a Service? And in what sense do Local Government officers constitute a Service to-day?

When we apply the term 'Service' to a body of men and women engaged in some particular occupation or employment, there must be some content of meaning in the term which goes beyond the obvious indication that these men and women collectively discharge some function in our social economy. We speak of the Army, the Navy and the Air Force as the Defence Services, but we have not hitherto spoken of the Leather Service or the Chemical Service. We had begun to speak of the Railway Service even before the nationalization of the railways, but we have not yet come to speak of the staff or workmen of Lever Bros. as the Soap Service. Some would say that we must look for the characteristics of a service in a common employer, and not merely common employment, and in some consequential ordering of the employees into a hierarchy, or an integrated organization, in which they assume a liability to be posted to this, that, or the other seat of duty. Such a narrow definition would exclude not only the Local Government Service but the Teaching and the Police Services. Local Government officers are not in the employ of one single employer. They fall into recognizable categories, categories which are in fact recognized by their individual employers, but there is no complete uniformity either in the duties or the remuneration of officers in the same category or holding the same titular rank. Nor, although Local Government officers are mobile in the sense that they can move from one employer to another, can they be posted by one employer to the service of another.

The essentials of popular meaning in the term 'Service',

and the propriety of its application to Local Government officers, rest on rather broader considerations than those referred to. To apply no other test than the usage of everyday speech, we would say that the term 'Service' comes to be applied to a body of employees when, no matter what differences exist between them in grade or individual occupation, they constitute one corps which serves some social or political institution, or collectively discharges some social function, and when, at the same time, they conform to some public expectation of standards in ability, training, and conduct. It is the public expectation of standards which seems to be the key to the usage of the term. Hence the reason why the term is not, and need not be, restricted to bodies of public servants. For example, we speak of the Merchant Service.

The public expectation of standards may sometimes be translated into requirements which have literally or virtually the force of law. Such, for example, are the requirements for Board of Trade certificates, for ships' officers; and the tests under railway legislation for certain classes of railway servant. But even when legal requirements are absent, we find that all occupational groups to which the term 'Service' is applied are marked by some common characteristics; and if in turn we examine these we can trace their development to a demand for standards.

The acquisition of standards by an occupational group may proceed in many different ways. It may be the result of some initiative or impetus on the part of the public themselves. Or the initiative and the impetus may come from the employees, as it did in the case of the Local Government Service. But in whatever way it is actuated the movement for standards produces some common lineaments in the occupational group concerned. Among these we find standards of ethical or occupational conduct, orderly methods of recruitment, standards of entry, standards of training, and standards of qualification. Complementary to these, we find the development of minimum or standard levels of remuneration, classification and grading of staff in levels or ranges of remuneration related to their occupation or function, the development of common service conditions, either for the group as a whole or particular grades and levels of it, and orderly procedures for dealing with promotion.

If characteristics such as these develop, the occupation may be accorded a certain status in the eyes of the public, and, apart from any particular standards due to itself, the public will expect the employees to maintain disciplined conduct and the employers to accord certain freedoms to their servants, such as freedom from arbitrary dismissal or from persecution by superiors. The totality of all these features may bring the Service to the point when the careers and prospects that it offers are matters of public note; and are known to, or can be made known to, the public, to every section of the personnel of the Service itself, to the would-be entrant, and to those who advise parents, scholars, apprentices and students on the choice of suitable careers.

If these be the characteristics of a Service, then we can say that Local Government officers indubitably constitute a Service to-day, tardy as the achievement of such a status has been, and much room as there may yet be for development and improvement. It is the object of this chapter to trace the forces and events which brought this situation about.

Early Conditions

We must begin by saying that well into the early years of this century practically all of the characteristics we have recited were lacking. For appointment to some of the chief officers' posts, the majority of the larger but only a minority of the smaller Local Authorities would look for such qualifications as were then current. The office of Town Clerk was usually filled by a solicitor, though often, in all but the largest towns, on a part-time basis from among local private practitioners. The office of Medical Officer was required by the Central Authority to be filled by a duly qualified medical practitioner. But few civil engineers and few chartered accountants were attracted by the Service in the earlier years; and it was not until the early years of the century that the establishment of the Institution of Municipal and County Engineers, and of the Institute of Municipal Treasurers and Accountants, brought about a qualification for the posts of

Surveyor and Treasurer, respectively. Some of the chief professional assistants to the Town Clerk, the Surveyor, and the Treasurer would be found to have qualifications similar to those of their chiefs. The majority of Local Government officers were, however, without qualifications of any kind. In the growing volume and pressure of work, members of the clerical classes were assuming responsibilities of an administrative kind, some of them very considerable; and apart from the absence of any specific qualification suited to administrative responsibility, the standard of education of these officers was usually deficient. The clerical classes as a whole were in fact recruited without any standards of education on entry.

It is possible to exaggerate the evils of this situation. Despite their deficiencies, many unqualified men in technical posts had had considerable practical experience, and many of them, together with many of the clerks who assumed administrative responsibilities, did, in fact, display remarkable adaptability. The situation was one which gave an opportunity to natural talents, even though these were unaccompanied by 'paper qualifications'.

On the other hand, there was a dead-weight of inefficient staff through the widespread evil of nepotism. Only a few Local Authorities, such as the London County Council, Middlesex, and Manchester, had inaugurated tests for entry on a competitive basis. The situation in the country at large was that clerical juniors (and in many places chief officers) secured their appointments through patronage. Political and religious elements in the local communities contended for a share of this patronage through their representatives on the Council. Political and religious influence, or favouritism, were similarly at work in the determination of salaries, and the filling of offices by promotion. In one place or another this situation led from time to time to charges and counter-charges by one party or faction against another, and the resulting publicity did good. But in some places it led to tacit understandings for patronage to be shared, so that its roots struck all the deeper.

No code of ethics for Local Government officers had

evolved which had any organized backing by either employers or employees; and while many and perhaps most Local Government officers showed, in conditions of great difficulty, standards of integrity and loyalty to the public interest which were beyond praise, the number of 'scandals' which came to light during the course of the nineteenth and the early years of the twentieth century was not an insignificant one and left an impression of widespread moral taint.

Not only were there no national, or even provincial, standards of remuneration, or common conditions of service, but even individual Local Authority grading schemes were largely unknown. There were chief officers who in those days enjoyed salaries relatively larger than those which are the rule to-day. The lot of their subordinates—the vast mass of clerical workers—was deplorable. The standards were those of the lowest types of commercial employment. And while many of the clerks were little removed from the condition of Bob Cratchit, scratching their pens in dingy, ill-ventilated and ill-lighted offices, too often they affected a spurious gentility, aped the airs of their social superiors, regarded themselves as far removed from the masses of the people because they 'worked in the town hall', and treated the humbler citizens of their local community with scant courtesy and little human understanding.

There were no facilities for post-entry training, and, for the rank-and-file, few inducements to it. There was no Superannuation Scheme, and this circumstance, combining with the absence of standard grading schemes, meant that mobility in the Service, one of the factors which makes so much for its efficiency, was practically nil. Staffs were largely 'inbred', and conditions thus rendered the more propitious for nepotism, patronage, and the unduly close personal relationships between Councillors and officers which were so often the seed-bed of malpractice.

The truth of the picture we have presented could be attested by many citations from the author's own early experience; but if any objective testimony is required, we may find it in what was perhaps the first independent survey ever made of the Local Government Service. This was the Fabian tract *From Patronage to Proficiency in the Public Service* by W. A. Robson, who now holds the Chair of Public Administration in London University. It appeared in 1922. Like most Fabian pamphlets, it was well documented and based on close factual survey, and it confirms the picture presented here. It examined standards of proficiency in the Civil Service as well as among Local Government officers, but its major purpose was obviously to draw attention to the important functions being discharged by Local Government, to point out how far the calibre of the rank-and-file staffs engaged in it then lagged behind that of the Civil Service, and to set before the public mind the need for the corps of Local Government officers to be moulded into a 'Service' in much the same sense as adduced in these pages. The machinery and methods through which a Local Government Service has at last been established are not precisely those which Professor Robson visualized thirty years ago; but no man more clearly saw the needs of the situation than he did. His tract did much to create a climate of public opinion favourable to subsequent endeavour, and must be accounted the first important document in the history of the Local Government Service.

It must have been very difficult for anyone at that epoch to visualize the means by which so great a transformation might be effected. The task might well have appeared impossible to those best able to measure it, but who were soon to set themselves the task of achieving it, namely, the Local Government officers themselves. Let us consider for a moment the barriers which lay in their path. The number of Local Authorities was greater than it is even to-day, when, as we have seen, it is 1,500, excluding the Parish authorities. Each one of them worked as an isolated unit. Few of them, as we have said, had got to the point of even formulating grading schemes or salary scales for their own staffs, or indeed any kind of orderly system of recruitment or personnel management. There were wide divergencies in conditions of service, even as between Authorities of the same kind in the same localities. Local Authorities were unconscious of any need for uniformities which would lay a foundation for mobility, and thus widen their field of choice in making appointments, and produce a flow of candidates with experience in more than one place. The outlook of the Local Authorities did but reflect the conditions of the time. In industry at large, the scope of collective bargaining was nothing like it is to-day. The idea of collective bargaining for employees such as Local Government officers was repugnant to prevailing sentiment. Trade unionism amongst the staffs themselves was as yet unborn. No impetus came from the public, because the public remained largely unconscious of the extent to which Local Government had already developed, and few foresaw what responsibilities would be given to it after 1918. Although the major portion of the field of public service at that time was in the hands of Local Authorities, and this situation rested upon parliamentary decisions in one form or another, Parliament and the Central Government remained indifferent to the need for a fashioned instrument of democratic Local Government such as the Civil Service was becoming in the central sphere. This attitude could even be justified on theoretical grounds. The Local Authorities should be left to manage their own affairs in their own way; and freedom to settle unilaterally the quality and conditions of their own staffs would seem to that day and generation perhaps the most conspicuous of the freedoms and discretions which they should exercise.

Trade Unionism as a Moulding Force

The impetus came from the staff themselves, and first expressed itself in a movement by various categories of Local Government officer to establish their own institutes for conferring qualifications by examination. Some of these institutes were already well established by the time when Professor Robson wrote his tract; and, as he said in reviewing them, 'the desire to abolish patronage and to improve the status of the various grades by eliminating the untrained (was) the chief motive compelling the members of practically all the brain-working grades in local administration to set up barriers against haphazard entry into their

various vocations'. Many of these qualifications remain
to-day, and, judged by present standards, some of them may
be deemed rather narrow and unduly specialized; some, in
fact, have been something of an embarrassment in the more
recent efforts made, with existing machinery, to attain
broader and more suitable kinds of qualification. Looking at
them broadly, however, we must agree with the remark of
Sidney and Beatrice Webb which Professor Robson cites in
reviewing them, 'that whatever may be the reason for professional organization among the brain-working officials of Local
Authorities, we suggest that it has been an almost unmixed
good, whilst its fuller recognition would be a further gain'.

But even these early endeavours left the vast mass of the
Service untouched; and, in any event, a radical improvement of service conditions, not to speak of any wider ambi-
tions for the establishment of a true Service, was obviously
a task going far beyond the limited aims of the professional
institutes. The next phase came with the establishment of
trade unionism, and in the light of subsequent events we may
say that trade unionism for Local Government staffs began
with the formation, in 1905, of the National Association of
Local Government Officers. From the outset this organization made its field of recruitment Local Government officers
as such, i.e. officers of all occupations and grades, from the
Town Clerk to his junior, stopping short only of the manual
workers. It has in fact succeeded in uniting in its ranks all
but a very small percentage of officers of all grades, though
it has never sought the enforcement of trade-union membership as a condition of Local Authority employment.

By the very nature of its objectives, i.e. standard conditions
of employment, trade unionism in any form was bound, to
the extent that it was successful, to go some way in the
direction of producing a Service out of a congeries of locally
appointed officers. The Local Government Service is indeed
primarily a creation of Local Government trade unionism;
it is also worth while noting that this could hardly have
happened if trade unionism itself had developed a structure
and policy different from those exemplified in N.A.L.G.O.
The very idea of a Service could not have become a cogent

ideal or an object of organized, sustained and comprehensive endeavour without the unity of spirit and the integrated policies which sprang from the voluntary association of so many diverse levels and groups of officers in the one organization. Had trade unionism developed through the formation of separate unions for different layers or groups, it is doubtful whether a Service could have evolved as soon as it did, late as in many ways this was. Nor could the Service have attained standards such as those of today had N.A.L.G.O. not embraced the training, education and qualification of the Local Government officer as an essential part of its trade union policy and pursued it with a vigour greater, not less, than that shown by the employing authorities.

It was the difficulty of finding or creating a national body, representative of employers, with which the staffs could deal through their own national organisation, which accounts for most of the delay in the advent of a Service; but by a process protracted throughout the period between the two world wars the employing authorities and the staffs were at last brought together in a standing machinery of 'collective bargaining', fashioned upon the lines advocated in the famous report of the Committee on Relations between Employers and Employees (the Whitley Report) of 1917. It is the decisions arrived at by this machinery which have now produced, or are now producing, the standards and arrangements characteristic of a true Service.

It can be said, then, that the Service is the product of Whitleyism. This is a fact and it is one of some significance in the history of 'industrial relations', for few in earlier days would have thought that any kind of Service could have originated without some large measure of legislative prescription. But it remains true that the Service is the product of trade unionism, for in the Local Government world Whitleyism itself, or at any rate the machinery which embodies its aim and spirit, is the product of trade unionism. The policy of the trade union concerned, i.e. N.A.L.G.O., was to seek its objectives along the lines of Whitley principles and through Whitley machinery and practice; and if to-day the Local Authorities, as employers, are willing participants in the Whitley machinery it is largely because of trade-union pressure, educative effort, and missionary spirit. Since education, training, and qualification, are within its scope, as well as pay, conditions of service, and standards of conduct, the Whitley machinery for the Local Government Service is probably unique in the ambit of the responsibilities which both sides have accorded to it.

N.A.L.G.O.'s first tasks were the first tasks of all trade unions—organization and recognition, i.e. the recruitment of employees not hitherto 'organized', and the recognition of the Association by the Local Authorities as a negotiating agency. We need not detail the stages of this preliminary effort, which in the circumstances of the time frequently met with much opposition from the employers. Suffice it to say that at the close of the First World War the Association had attained an appreciable membership, and that after the industrial unrest of 1911–14, and the further labour troubles of the war period, public opinion grew more and more favourable to collective bargaining and trade-union organization, and that the opposition of 'reactionary' councils to trade-union organization for their staffs was gradually worn down.

As to service conditions objectives, there were, in the period from 1905 to 1918, two. One of them did much to establish the Association as a national organization, namely, legislation to enable Local Authorities to establish schemes of superannuation for their officers. The position at that time was that Local Authorities had no power to establish such schemes, or even to make payments by way of pension out of their rate revenue, the assignment of any penny of public revenue towards retiring allowances being *ultra vires*. N.A.L.G.O.'s pursuit of a remedy for this state of affairs did much in itself to unite chief officers and rank and file in the one national organization. Such an aim could obviously only be effectively pursued on a national plane. It was pursued through parliamentary lobbying, interviews with Ministers and officials of Government Departments, and by propaganda among the members of the Local Authorities themselves and leading citizens throughout the country. The effort proved to be a protracted one and brought no fruit until 1922, when the Local Government Superannuation Act of that year enabled any Local Authority to establish superannuation funds and schemes on lines prescribed by the Act, if it so decided. Quite a number of Authorities did so decide, but not until 1937 did a compulsory measure eventuate in the shape of the Local Government Superannuation Act of that year.

The other service conditions objective related to pay, and had to be pursued by local negotiation on the part of the Association's officers—mostly voluntary officers at branch level helped by a small paid field staff—the negotiations being primarily directed, from the staff side, to the establishment of grading schemes and associated scales of pay. This arduous effort, pursued on the wide front of about 1,500 to 2,000 individual Authorities, in the absence of any standing machinery for collective bargaining at wider levels, had made little headway before 1914. It was only a handful of Authorities, and those the larger, which had established grading schemes, and in all of these there were extraordinary disparities.

The work and influence of the Association received an undoubted impetus, and recruitment into its ranks was greatly stimulated, when it succeeded, in 1919, in procuring for Local Government officers a cost-of-living bonus on uniform lines awarded to the Civil Service. Like other classes of public servants, Local Government officers sustained the impact of the tremendous rise in the cost of living during the first years of the war with practically no compensating increase in remuneration. While most Local Authorities had been forced to make substantial concessions to the manual workers under trade-union pressure, either by way of increased wages or 'war bonuses' related to cost-of-living figures, few of them had done anything for their official staffs. The award itself (No. 84) was ludicrously inadequate, and even when it was followed by further awards or agreements a year or two later the salaried staffs were still lagging behind the manual workers in the augmentation of pay. The fact remained

E

that these awards were the first visible sign to Local Government staffs in general of what they stood to gain from trade-union organization capable of deploying itself at national levels.

Meanwhile, the Association had been active in the other aspects of its policy—the education and training of the Service—and had established in the year 1912 an examination for non-professional staffs. Under advice from friendly circles in the teaching world and the Civil Service, the examination developed a fairly high standard, with intermediate and final stages. The Authorities began to take it into account in considering the promotion of officers, and to award grants to their officers who succeeded in passing it. But in resorting to this measure the Association realized that it was resorting only to what was possible in the circumstances of the time. Its own feeling was that qualifications ought to be conferred by bodies other than the trade union to which the officers belonged. Nor did the Association over-emphasize the place and value of the Correspondence Institute which it established some years later, i.e. in 1919. In the developments of recent years, the Association's examination has been abandoned, but its Correspondence Institute continues in full vigour, has fulfilled a useful rôle in providing facilities for specialized examinations, and has widened its scope so as to fill some of the gaps in teaching facilities for the broader type of qualifications and promotion tests which are established to-day. Broadly speaking, however, even in these earlier years the Association had arrived at the view, not only that the universities should be induced to interest themselves in qualifications at the higher level, but that in some way the Local Authorities must also be brought in to the many-sided task of education and training, though it was some years before the Association saw the potentialities of Whitleyism in the second of these objectives.

The Beginnings of Whitleyism

At the close of the First World War public opinion was considerably influenced by the Whitley Report. In so far as the suggestions made in this report envisaged a fuller resort to collective bargaining, they were hardly novel. What was novel in them was the plea for the establishment of standing machinery in which organizations of the employers and of employees would participate in a regular and continuous address to the adjustment of employer-and-employee relationship. Behind this policy was the conviction that neither side should wait until trouble arose, and then attempt to allay it by the sporadic negotiation which proved so difficult for both trade-union or employers' organizations when unilateral action had already been taken by one or the other, or when particular groups of workers or employers had already kicked over the traces at some action, conduct, or attitude on the part of the other. There was, too, a further feature in the policy put forward in the Whitley report which represented a considerable development in the practice of collective bargaining, i.e. that the representatives of the two sides should act as representatives in the fullest sense, and not merely delegates, and that they should be so chosen and appointed, under the constitution of the representative machinery, as to be accepted as plenipotentiaries with power to effect a settlement, at any rate by a majority vote of each of the two sides. In collective bargaining as previously practised the negotiators on either side were usually only in the position of delegates, and obliged to refer back to their constituents before agreement was reached.

It is this second feature which to-day constitutes the essential feature of Whitleyism; since, in most fields, collective bargaining now rests upon some kind of standing machinery. Not every body of employers or employees accepts the essential Whitley principle in negotiating practice. Some unions have never favoured Whitleyism as a policy, and it may, indeed, be that its application is more difficult in some fields than in others. Experiments in its application took place on a wide scale in the years immediately following the First World War, but by no means all of them succeeded.

Such an experiment took place in the field of Local Government in 1919, following upon conversations between representatives of N.A.L.G.O. and of the Local Authority associations.   As a first experiment it was only partially successful. A National Joint Council was formed, but it withered away a few years later without having accomplished anything more substantial and lasting than a demarcation of areas for the operation of Provincial Councils as a second tier of the complete structure. Efforts at provincial level were more successful, and Provincial Councils struck root in three areas, Lancashire and Cheshire, Yorkshire, and London. Of these, the most effective was that in Lancashire and Cheshire. Working independently in its own area with the support of N.A.L.G.O. and a nucleus of Local Authority membership on the employers' side, it evolved salary scales and conditions of service for Local Authorities' staffs in the area, and made recommendations on standards of entry and procedures for orderly recruitment, and a variety of other matters. Before the outbreak of the Second World War, it had attracted the majority of Local Authorities in the area into membership; and, while it had no powers over constituent Local Authority members in the matter of grading, within the framework of the agreed salary scales, many of the Local Authorities had begun to consult it on such questions, and in this way a useful approach was made to the establishment of uniformities in the evaluation of particular posts and well-defined classes of work. It may be said indeed that the Lancashire and Whitley Council showed not only that Whitleyism was inherently suitable to the Local Government field, but convinced those associated with it that the scope of Whitleyism in this field could be even greater and wider than questions of pay and service conditions. Moreover, in many matters of constitution, procedure, and practice, it not only consolidated its own functions and influence, but evolved an invaluable pattern for later extensions of Whitleyism throughout the provincial level, and for the eventual re-establishment of a National Joint Council.

But for many years progress elsewhere was slow. Not yet were Local Authorities as a whole wedded to the idea of Whitleyism. Many Local Authorities viewed with doubt a policy which would take away their individual independence and autonomy even in one aspect of the employer and employee relationship. On the other hand, the Local Government officers' trade union, N.A.L.G.O., despite the disappointment of its earlier hopes, and an ensuing phase, by no means unnatural, of misgiving and doubt as to the feasibility or the wisdom of the Whitley line of policy, eventually came down decisively in favour of it. From the nineteen-thirties onwards, all the energies of the Association were deployed to the establishment of a complete national system of Whitley Councils, first at the provincial level, and as soon as possible at the national level, with local joint staff committees as their complement on the local plane.

The Hadow Report

In 1934 N.A.L.G.O.'s work was powerfully aided by the appearance of the Report of the Hadow Departmental Committee on the qualifications, recruitment, training and promotion of Local Government officers. The appointment of the Departmental Committee had been suggested by the Royal Commission on Local Government, which sat from 1923 till 1929. The Commission was primarily concerned with questions of Local Government structure, but took notice of the general state of affairs in regard to the recruitment and appointment of Local Government officers, and the expectation which the public might have as to the standards of service which should be given by the staffs to their Authorities, and through them to the public. The Committee suggested a number of questions which might be looked into in detail by a departmental committee, and Mr. Arthur Greenwood, while Minister of Health in 1930, appointed a Committee under the chairmanship of Sir Henry Hadow, with terms of reference to enquire into, and make recommendations on, the qualifications, recruitment, training and promotion of Local Government officers. This report represented the first survey ever undertaken on the nation's behalf of a group of public servants whose ministrations had been growing more important and more extensive every year throughout the preceding century or so. If Professor Robson's pamphlet was the first document which finds a place in the history of the Local Government Service, and if the Whitley Report can be accounted the second, the Hadow Report is to be accounted the third. We need not go into the detail of the report. It undoubtedly revealed an improvement in the general calibre and standards of Local Government officers since the state of affairs surveyed by Professor Robson. It acknowledged that in the main 'the Local Government Service' maintained a high standard. For the first time in an official document it used the term 'Local Government Service', perhaps a little prematurely, but, nevertheless, in unmistakable testimony to the conditions which were developing and the needs which had now arisen. It paid a tribute to what the associations of officers had done to raise the standards of their services. It acknowledged that it had been favourably impressed by the evidence given on their behalf (which was given by N.A.L.G.O. and a number of the professional associations associated with it). 'We ourselves,' said the Committee, 'owe these associations our thanks for the assistance which they have given to us.' Nevertheless, as the reports show, some of the defects stressed by Professor Robson in the earlier years still remained, and the general tenor of the Committee's report was that the expansion of Local Government, and the public expectation that it should be efficiently served, called for improvement. The general gist of the report can be seen from the Committee's own summary of the recommendations they made. These are as follows:

RECRUITMENT

General Considerations and Proposals

1. Notification of vacancies.—All vacancies should be widely notified, except where it is intended to fill them by promotion inside the office.

2. Selection.—Candidates should ordinarily be interviewed by a committee of the Council; selection by an officer should be exceptional.

3. Disqualification of interested persons.—The candidature of near relations of members or officers should be closely scrutinized, members, officers and candidates being required to disclose relationship.

4. Canvassing should invariably disqualify a candidate.

5. Probation.—All newcomers to the Service should be appointed on a term of probation, should be thoroughly tested, and should be appointed to the established staff only if reports are satisfactory.

6. Security of tenure.—Before a senior officer is dismissed, notice should be given to all members of the Authority, and, if the officer so requests, the notice should state the grounds of the complaint.

7. Employment by authority.—Local Authorities should not authorize their officers to appoint and pay their own assistants, but should be directly responsible for the appointment and salary of every member of their staff.

Junior Clerical Officers

8. Minimum qualifications.—Sixteen years should be the minimum age for entry, and a school certificate the minimum educational qualification. Vacancies should be open to girls as well as to boys.

9. Recruitment from a higher age group.—Local Authorities should recruit a certain proportion of junior clerical officers at eighteen or nineteen years of age, the larger Local Authorities making systematic arrangements to do so.

10. Method of recruiting clerical officers.—Junior clerical officers should preferably be recruited by open competitive examination, neighbouring Local Authorities combining for the purpose.

University Graduates

11. University graduates should be systematically recruited by the larger Local Authorities; and there should be central machinery for the selection of this type of candidate. Competitive examination is recommended.

Professional and Technical Officers

12. Field of recruitment.—In recruiting their professional and technical officers, Local Authorities should look to all available sources, whether inside or outside the Service.

13. Articled pupilage.—No premium should be required from pupils articled to officers; and the selection of pupils by officers should be subject to the Authority's approval.

Qualifications of Principal Officers

14. Clerks.—The essential qualification of a Clerk is administrative ability; a legal qualification may be convenient, but should not be insisted on to the exclusion of persons of proved administrative ability who do not possess the qualification.

To secure that sufficient officers of administrative ability are available, Local Authorities should broaden the basis of recruitment, provide training in administration for junior officers, and encourage the study of the principles of administration.

15. Other principal officers.—No radical change in the existing system of requiring principal officers to possess technical qualifications is suggested, but more attention should be paid to administrative ability and experience.

16. Subordinate administrative officers.—Large Authorities might consider the appointment of responsible administrative assistants to the principal officers.

TRAINING AND PROMOTION

Grades and Salary Scales

17. Every Local Authority should adopt a scheme of grading and salary scales. The grades of different Authorities should as far as possible be comparable.

Variety of Experience

18. Selected clerical officers should be given experience of different departments. Freer movement of clerical officers between different Authorities is also desirable, and senior clerical vacancies should ordinarily be advertised. Universal superannuation schemes are required.

The Use of Examinations

19. An examination bar.—Local Authorities should require junior officers to pass a qualifying examination before they will be considered eligible for promotion from the general grade.

20. Nature of the examinations.—The examinations qualifying officers for promotion from the general grade should be either the first part of a recognized technical examination, or an administrative examination. Local Authorities should combine to secure that an administrative examination of suitable standard is available.

Promotion

21. Method of promotion.—Principal officers should keep records of the progress of all officers in their department, and these records should be referred to the appropriate committee if the officer is either unusually promising or not up to standard.

22. Grants, increments, special leave.—Grants, or increments might be made to officers obtaining approved qualifications. Grants might also be made to educational institutions providing approved courses, on condition that selected officers are allowed to attend. Special leave should be granted in exceptional cases.

Technical Qualifications

23. Several questions arise and a thorough investigation is required. The investigation should be carried out by a central body, representative of Local Authorities.

GENERAL CONCLUSIONS

Establishment Committees

24. All questions affecting the recruitment, qualifications, training and promotion of officers, should be assigned to a central committee in every Local Authority.

A Central Advisory Committee

25. The principal need of the Service is a standing body charged with the supervision of all questions affecting officers. The associations of Local Authorities and the London County Council should combine to appoint a standing committee for this purpose.

The report exerted a considerable influence in official circles—Parliament, the Government, the Universities, and the Local Authorities. N.A.L.G.O. accepted it and took steps to bring its import home to every Local Authority in the country. The Government brought the terms of the report to the notice of the Local Authorities in an official circular, but no official action followed beyond that. More could hardly have been expected unless opinion had moved, as fortunately it did not, in the direction of imposing the recommendations by central prescription of some kind.

The report had not dealt directly with pay and conditions, but only standards of proficiency. For the realization of many of its recommendations on qualifications and training, the report proposed the establishment of a Central Advisory Committee; but although N.A.L.G.O. accepted the report, its own view was that these objectives could be better pursued as one phase in the functions of a comprehensive Whitleyism. It felt that questions of training and qualification could not be divorced from questions of pay and conditions, and that little indeed might be accomplished unless the weight of Whitley organization and authority could be brought to bear on one set of questions in

conjunction with the other. The Committee's suggestion for
an *ad hoc* advisory committee was rooted perhaps in two considerations: first, the fact that Whitleyism was in 1934 by
no means universally established, and the Committee would
be going beyond its terms of reference in suggesting a machine
which would deal with other subjects than those of training
and qualification; second, that questions relating to standards
should be divorced from the process of bargaining and compromise inherent in Whitleyism. N.A.L.G.O. saw the force
of this latter argument, but believed that a place could be
found within the Whitley constitution for some kind of
independent tribunal capable of dealing with qualifications
without bringing them into the atmosphere of bargain and
compromise that necessarily surrounded negotiation for pay.
We shall see, later on, how the issue was resolved. What we
have to note here is that the advisory committee was never
in fact established. The most powerful of the Local Authority
associations, namely, the Association of Municipal Corporations, was not prepared to accept the proposal. It is difficult
to see why. It was certainly not because the Association
preferred N.A.L.G.O.'s solution, because not yet had the
Association or, for that matter, the other associations of
Local Authorities, given a blessing to the policy of Whitleyism for the Local Government Service, despite a gradual
but fairly substantial orientation of Local Authority opinion
in that direction. The report, however, set up goals for all
concerned, widened N.A.L.G.O.'s own vision of the scope
which Whitleyism might have, and encouraged it not a little
to develop and strengthen that side of its policy which
studied the public interest and sought standards of efficiency
as a necessary condition of fair service conditions.

The Completion of the Whitley Edifice

From 1935 to the outbreak of the Second World War
the Association's policy registered increasing success by the
establishment of further provincial councils in parts of the
country where they had hitherto been unknown. Most
of the newly formed bodies proceeded to the settlement of
provincial scales and schemes of classification, standards of

entry, and like matters. When the war broke out, the chain
of Provincial Councils was almost but not quite complete.
It was, in fact, completed a year or two later in the difficult
conditions of wartime.

In 1936 an attempt was made to revive the National Joint
Council. The Council came into being, and functioned,
finding after 1939, in the years of war, a task ready to its
hand in the formulation of schemes for cost-of-living adjustments of salary as the cost of living mounted. But this Council,
too, looked like foundering within a few years of its establishment; though in retrospect it might be said that its potentialities for wider functions were being surveyed and tested, and
that this was a hopeful sign in itself, even though in the event
it was found wanting as the major instrument of a developed
Whitleyism. The Local Authorities, or rather some of their
associations, found impediments in its constitution, or, to
be more precise, in the basis of representation on its employers' side. The objections mostly came from the larger
Authorities, who feared that although they were the largest
employers their interests would be overwhelmed by the large
number of small Authorities, in view of the representation
these could carry on the employers' side under the existing
constitution. There was some justification in these objections.
On the other hand, Local Authorities being as varied in type
and size, and as numerous, as they were, it was no easy
matter to find a solution. This time, however, there were
leaders among the employers, as well as among the staffs, who
were determined to secure the establishment of a comprehensive Whitley machine, because they knew this to be the
only solution to the situation which would face Local
Government after the war. The solution was eventually
found by dividing the representation on the employers' side
as between direct representatives of the Local Authority
associations and representatives of Provincial Councils, it
being contemplated that Provincial Councils would be a
constituent part of the machine as a whole, and that an
orderly relationship should be established between them and
the National Joint Council. On the employers' side the
Provincial Councils would continue to be representative of

all the constituent Local Authorities within the Provincial area, either by appointment of representatives of each or by election of representatives from each group of Authorities of the same kind. The arrangement was one which at one and the same time provided a guaranteed representation for the type of Authority most liable to have been 'submerged', i.e. the County Councils, while in other respects it ensured a fairly mixed representation. Upon this new representative basis the National Joint Council was reconstituted by agreement between the Local Authority associations and the staff organizations, and came into existence in 1944–5. The scope and functions of the new body were conceived of comprehensively and expressed in wide terms, on the basis of a division of work and responsibilities as between the National Councils and the Provincial Councils. In this latter respect a fundamental change had occurred. The foundations for a comprehensive machine had unquestionably been laid at the Provincial level by piecemeal process. This process had meant that in each area the Provincial Council went as far as practice had evolved in the collective bargain between employers and staff. Under the new system, the National Joint Council would assume the functions of settling on the national plane the main framework of conditions for application throughout the Service; and in the main, the task of the Provincial Council in future would be to see to the application of the National Council's schemes. Having done so much, as independent bodies, in devising schemes of their own for application in their own areas, it is not unnatural that some elements on the employers' side of the Provincial Councils were perturbed at the secondary level of responsibility which would mark their rôle in future. But at last the Local Authority associations had come down heavily in favour of a policy of establishing national conditions for the Service, and it was largely by their influence that difficulties were overcome, the new Constitution passed, and steps taken immediately to give the new National Joint Council the task of framing a national scheme.

A national scheme was eventually, and, in fact, with commendable speed, agreed on 30th January 1946. This is the scheme which is known throughout the Service and among the Local Authorities as the 'Charter'.

We shall describe the main features of this Scheme in the next chapter. We may note here that its comprehensive nature is indicated by the sections into which it is divided, dealing with recruitment and training, conditions of service, salary scales, classification and grading of staff, and the conduct of officers. In one way or another, if not always in the precise way envisaged by the Hadow Committee, all the substantive recommendations of that Committee were implemented in the Charter, or are being progressively applied in the practice which has developed under it.

When it agreed upon the National Scheme of Conditions of Service, the National Joint Council also decided to establish a Local Government Examinations Board. The primary function to be allotted to the Board was to devise and manage the Promotions Examination contemplated by the Scheme as the condition for promotion from the basic grade (except where the officer possesses or acquires a professional or technical qualification, or some other qualification recognized as an equivalent or alternative to the Promotions Examination), and to advise the National Joint Council as to the facilities to enable candidates to prepare for this examination. In respect of this primary function, the Board is independent. Since the Board was established, soon after the Charter, the National Joint Council has conferred upon it further functions of an advisory character. It is to keep under general review the examinations which affect the Local Government Service; to advise the National Joint Council upon the arrangements necessary to implement from time to time the provisions of the Charter relating to the appointment of juniors, the admission of recruits at higher age groups, and the admission of university graduates; and is given a general reference to consider 'any matter referred to it by the National Joint Council'. The Board is a composite body, with personnel drawn partly from that of the National Joint Council and partly from exterior resources. The Board very quickly devised a Promotions Examination, but we shall comment on this examination and subsequent developments in the later chapters on Qualifications and Training.

The National Joint Council was established to deal with staffs up to a salary level of £700 a year. This 'ceiling' was fixed at the instance of the employers, who felt that the machine could appropriately deal with, and regulate on some basis of uniformity, the conditions for officers up to that level, while leaving the Local Authorities free to handle on an individual footing staffs above that level. Whitleyism thus stopped short of the chief officers and a considerable number of their principal subordinates. At the time when the National Joint Council was reconstituted and produced the Charter, the prevailing sentiment amongst the Local Authorities and their senior officers was undoubtedly against any attempt to establish uniformities at these higher levels, and, still more, to provide any machinery by which these might be secured. In a year or two, however, a remarkable shift of opinion took place towards collective bargaining for the higher levels of the Service. Argument then ensued as to whether the chief officers, and other officers at senior level, might be catered for by extending the scope of the National Joint Council or in some other way. Some felt that there should be an orderly relationship throughout the Service from the bottom to the top, and that difficulties would ensue if separate bodies were left to deal with different strata of the Service. Others felt that it would be improper for the conditions of chief officers or their seniors to be settled by the body which, on the staffs' side, must inevitably have a preponderance of representatives drawn from the lower and more numerous grades. The chief officers themselves had a very strong feeling that their interests should not be dealt with by a staff side which would of necessity be so largely representative of subordinate officers. Eventually, despite the rejoinder that special panels of the National Joint Council might be formed, with special representation and a large measure of autonomy, to deal with the upper grades of the Service, it was the 'separatist' view which prevailed.

Argument then took place as to what classes of officer should be dealt with by the proposed new machinery. The

arrangement eventually agreed upon did not please every-
one, but secured approval in or about 1947–8. It was based
on the establishment of two separate negotiating committees,
one known as Negotiating Committee A, for Clerks to Local
Authorities other than Clerks to County Councils (who some
years previously had entered into an informal machinery of
discussion with the County Councils Association). On this
Committee A the representation is drawn on the employers'
side from the Local Authority associations, and on the
staffs' side from the Society of Town Clerks, the Society of
Urban District Clerks, and the Society representing Rural
District Clerks. On this Committee N.A.L.G.O. has no
representation. Negotiating Committee A formulated agreements for conditions of service and for ranges of salary for
Clerks to Local Authorities, embodied in successive Recommendations dated 1949 and 1950.

The other body is called Negotiating Committee B. It was
established primarily to cater for specified groups of chief
officer, beginning with Treasurers, Engineers and Surveyors,
Chief Education Officers, and City and County Architects.
Its constitution provides that other groups of specified
officers may be later brought within the scope of the Committee by agreement. In addition, Negotiating Committee
B was given a jurisdiction in respect of all officers over
£1,000 a year, and as a concomitant step it was agreed by
the parties concerned that the level of the National Joint
Council's jurisdiction should be raised so as to extend to
officers up to a level of £1,000 a year. The scales of salary
agreed in the Charter were shortly afterwards extended by
the provision of two further scales bridging the gap between
the old ceiling of £700 and the new ceiling of £1,000 per
annum.

Negotiating Committee B took longer to arrive at any
settlement than did Committee A, but a scheme for ranges
of salary and service conditions for the four specified groups
of officers mentioned was agreed in October 1950. At the
time when these lines are written the further task remained
of dealing with the residual groups at existing levels of more
than £1,000 a year, and of co-ordinating what may be done

for these groups by Negotiating Committee B, and what may be done by the National Joint Council in the way of prescribing standardized gradings for any officers in these groups whose salaries are within that Council's ceiling. To this end a joint committee of the two bodies was appointed towards the end of 1950.

As yet, neither of the two negotiating committees mentioned has evolved the more formal and elaborate constitution characteristic of the National Joint Council. Their practice and procedure have still to be developed. In essence, however, they are Whitley bodies, and justify the statement which we can now make, that in 1951 a complete system of Whitleyism extends throughout the Local Government Service in England and Wales.

A separate National Joint Council for Scotland was constituted in 1937, following upon a conference of Scottish Local Authorities, and produced a Scottish Charter in 1947. In general shape this followed the lines of the English Charter agreed a year or so previously by the reconstituted National Joint Council for England and Wales. There are, however, some important differences, noted in the next chapter. In 1950 no separate machinery for chief officers had been established in Scotland, but arrangements for dealing with them were under discussion and it is understood that the Scottish Local Authorities favoured the principle of bringing them within the scope of the Joint Council with appropriate arrangements for the representation of their special interests. But with the exception of the development of machinery for chief officers it can be said that in Scotland, too, Whitleyism is fully established throughout the Service.

As we shall see, the Charter was a comprehensive scheme, designed both for immediate and continuing application according to the nature of its varied provisions. So far as standards of remuneration are concerned, it was founded upon a series of salary scales, and the application of these was conditioned to a process of grading individual posts, supplemented by a subsequent process of formulating, through the recommendations of the National Joint Council, uniform gradings for posts capable of that kind of treatment.

It took a few years, therefore, even to apply the Charter initially. In 1950, however, this process had got very near to completion, and the Charter was operative in all Local Authorities except for a few diminutive Authorities reliant upon part-time staffs, to which in the main the Charter was not applicable. The same was true of the Scottish Charter.

As regards the recommendations of Committees A and B, both committees had recommended that the scales and conditions agreed be applied immediately to officers who were within five years of superannuable age; and operative dates for other officers affected were agreed late in 1950.

Further work remains for Committee B in reviewing the position of officers over salary levels of £1,100 a year other than the 'specified' officers dealt with by the agreement just referred to. Some of these are in recognisable groups which also include officers below the £1,000 level and within the scope of the National Joint Council. In the latter part of 1950 a joint committee of the National Joint Council and Committee B was set up to review the position of these officers with a view to seeing whether any uniform gradings or scales could be established, or how best the officers could be dealt with on orderly lines.

We conclude by emphasizing what a long and arduous process the creation of a Local Government Service in the true sense of the term has been, and how difficult has been the task of building up the machinery which eventually brought such a service into existence.

There are many prominent men among the elected representatives in the Local Government world, and many in governmental academic and professional circles who have made notable contributions to so great an achievement, but the bulk of the credit is due to the leaders of a generation of Local Government officers which must shortly pass out of public service. It is to be hoped that the generation which follows them will have a sense of their faith and pioneering spirit, and be as ready as they were to serve the needs of to-day and to-morrow.

F

CHAPTER IV

National Service Conditions

THE CHARTER, in documentary form, incorporating subsequent interpretations and supplementary agreements for its detailed application, extends to some sixty octavo pages; and in reviewing it here we must concentrate upon its salient provisions and, in particular, those which have moulded the Service into its characteristic shape.

If the Charter, as a document, strikes the general reader as drawn in rather wide language, leaving much for later and continuing application, and if the extent to which it has called for subsequent interpretation is large, these circumstances are not surprising. A comprehensive approach to the ordering of a service so heterogeneous as the Local Government Service could obviously be no easy task—certainly one more difficult than that of dealing with the Civil Service, Teachers, or the Police—all of them homogeneous bodies in comparison with the Local Government Service. The surprising thing is that a scheme which did make so comprehensive an approach proved itself within comparatively so short a space of time to be effective in bringing about the very great changes which it contemplated. It comprises a Preamble, and five parts. Part I deals with Recruitment and Training; Part II with General Conditions of Service; Part III with Scales of Salaries; Part IV with Official Conduct; and Part V with Interpretation, Appeal, and other matters of application, some transitional.

The Preamble opens with a brief statement in general terms of the National Joint Council's scope and functions. It contains two important recommendations to Local Authorities, one for the setting up of Staff or Establishment committees, and the other for the introduction of Local Joint Committees representative of the Local Authority and its staff, both of which recommendations are discussed in a later chapter.

Recruitment and Training

In approaching Part I, dealing with Recruitment and Training, we should realize that it does not purport to prescribe exhaustively over the whole range of this subject. Rather does it comprise a number of specific provisions severally directed to securing the improvements which the negotiators thought to be most needed, and which the Council was free to seek at the levels of its jurisdiction. The recruitment and qualifications of chief officers, as such, are not dealt with. Nor are the qualifications of professional and technical staff. The provisions assume that Local Authorities would continue to seek appropriate qualifications on the footing of those which had come to be recognized in practice. And, similarly, the whole Charter presumes the continuance of the extensive practice which had developed between the two wars of making appointments 'from outside' after advertisement, as well as by promotion, and the continuance of the procedures associated with such competitive recruitment. Indeed, the very first provision of Part I is a declaratory one in the widest terms, i.e. 'in order to obtain the best qualified and most efficient service recruitment shall be from the widest possible field'.

The objects with which Part I was mostly concerned were the attainment of better standards of education and ability in junior entrants; the admission of new entrants at rather higher ages; and measures for post-entry training at all levels which would at one and the same time meet the interests of employers and employed by improving efficiency, ensuring an adequate flow of trained officers for higher responsibilities, and provide a ladder of opportunity for the serving officer. Curiously enough, one of the most important provisions relating to qualification and training in the whole Charter—perhaps the most important if we consider, as we shall do later on, all that is flowing from it—was not contained in Part I at all. This is the requirement for the passing of a Promotion Examination devised by the Local

Government Examinations Board as a condition of *eligibility* for promotion out of the General Division, i.e. the basic grade of the Service entered at junior level at sixteen with incremental progression according to age up to a prescribed maximum. This requirement appears in Part III as a condition to the National Scales of Salaries.

The provision for junior entry is as follows:

'The minimum age for appointment of a junior entrant to the Local Government Service shall normally be sixteen years of age. Entrance to the Service shall be by examination, such examination to be arranged by the employing Authority or, alternatively, by the Provincial Councils acting on behalf of any group or groups of employing Authorities, and shall consist of two stages: (1) a qualifying stage and (2) a competitive stage (including interview) to select from the field constituted under (1). The standard of the qualifying examination shall be not less than that in force under the School Certificate Examination.'

Changes in the educational system rendered the requirement of School Certificate obsolete, and on the other hand delayed the introduction of any substituted standard. The Local Government Service has, moreover, experienced the same post-war difficulties in the recruitment of juniors as other spheres of public service, for a variety of reasons. Authorities which had introduced competitive examinations before the Charter have continued to hold them. Such a course is not an easy one for small Authorities, and the intention that the Provincial Councils might conduct examinations for them was frustrated by the volume of work that descended upon them in the grading of staffs under Part II of the Charter and to their limited resources in part-time staff. The alternative arrangements since agreed are discussed in Chapter IX.

This paragraph of the Scheme is followed by one which declares that an appropriate proportion of junior officers should be recruited at about eighteen or nineteen years of age, subject to the second, i.e. the competitive, test applicable to entrance at the lower age, the intention being to dispense with the prior qualifying stage in the case of boys or girls who stay the extra two years or so at school after sixteen, many of them, of course, with the intention of taking the Higher School Certificate, or its current equivalent.

A further paragraph declares that the Service should have within its ranks persons holding university degrees, that adequate facilities should be afforded by the employing Authorities for serving officers to obtain qualifications of this kind, but that a limited number of university graduates must also be recruited direct. The intention of this paragraph seems to have been to open a door to university graduates other than professional officers (who often, of course, have a university qualification in addition to their professional qualification). The place for the non-professional graduate in Local Government is probably smaller, even on the pure merits of the question, than is imagined by some critics who have complained that little has been done in the implementation of this provision of the Scheme. However, this is a question to which we shall revert later on.

A further very important provision of the Scheme states that facilities for obtaining Articles of Pupilage shall be afforded to officers in the service of the employing Authority. For the full implementation of this provision much may still remain to be done, and it will have to be done by agreement with the Local Authorities, the professional chief officers, and the governing bodies of the professions to which they belong. For many years before the Charter, facilities of the kind mentioned had been more freely available than in the old days when not merely lack of means to pay premiums, stamp duties, and fees for tuition, but snobbery on the part of some chief officers and an ungenerous attitude on the part of some employing Councils denied the opportunity of advancement to the higher ranks of the Service to many a promising subordinate. To-day a new generation of chief officers is, on the whole, actuated by better sentiments, and some financial assistance may be available from the Local Authority under provisions later mentioned. If much remains to be done to apply fully the provision under review, it has, nevertheless, as a declaration of principle, had a helpful effect, and it sets up a goal for further effort.

A further article in this part of the Scheme recognizes that at all levels training may be afforded by variety of early experience, and provides as follows:

(a) Facilities should be provided for the training of juniors up to twenty-one years of age by transfer from one department to another.

(b) Selected clerical and administrative officers should be seconded to departments other than those in which they are serving, in order to obtain a wider administrative experience.

(c) Upon a vacancy arising in the establishment of any department of an employing Authority, the staff of each department should be notified of the vacancy and the conditions attaching to the appointment, and in the filling of the vacancy consideration should be given to applications received from officers in the employ of the Authority.

Since it postulates that a vacancy has arisen, there should be no great difficulty in applying paragraph (c), which was aimed at a habit of thought very prevalent in the past—that in filling vacancies by promotion only the staff of the particular department in which the vacancy occurred need be considered. Other things being equal, a departmental applicant with some knowledge of the department's work, and perhaps of the duties of the particular post which is vacant, will stand the best chance. But it is a stimulating condition that applicants from other departments should be given the opportunity to compete. In any event, the vacancy need not be filled from existing staff, for at all levels the Local Authority is free to advertise if it thinks that course desirable. The paragraphs relating to the mobility of juniors, and the secondment of officers from one department to another, are admirable in aim, though not always easy to apply when a department is under heavy pressure of work, or its functions are expanding. The application of these provisions is, indeed, a matter for Whitleyism at the local level, where the local administrative exigencies can be known, and the intentions of the paragraph pursued with due regard to them.

Part I of the Scheme concludes with the following important and comprehensive article providing for post-entry training:

'With a view to meeting the demands made by the increasing importance and the growth of the Local Government Service, it is essential that in addition to the qualification required at entry officers should continue their studies after entry into the Service, and arrangements on the following line shall be made by employing Authorities:

(1) Attendance at part-time classes approved by the employing Authority for the continuance of general education, with some approach to appropriate vocational studies, incorporating an elementary understanding of the principles of Local Government and public administration, should be required.

Where a junior officer has not already obtained the preliminary qualification appropriate to the technical, professional or administrative course for which he proposes eventually to study, he should be advised as to suitable classes for that purpose.

(2) Guidance and adequate facilities (including financial assistance if found necessary) should be provided by the employing Authority to enable officers, through an approved procedure, to obtain such professional or technical qualification as is appropriate to the branch of the service in which the officer is engaged.

(3) Guidance and adequate facilities (including financial assistance if found necessary) should be provided by the employing Authority to enable officers in approved cases to proceed to a University Degree or Diploma in Public Administration. In special circumstances, it is suggested that selected officers should be seconded to University full-time courses, on agreement to return to the employing Authority for not less than a period to be specified.

(4) Officers should be encouraged to undertake systematic and regulated study of Local Government and its problems, and in order to ensure this being done employing Authorities should consider the organisation of courses of study, lectures, library facilities, and facilities for research.

(5) Any scheme of post-entry training under the above proposals should come within the purview of a Local Joint Committee, representative of the employing Authority and the staff, or, in the absence of such joint committee, the establishment committee of the employing authority, in consultation with representatives of the staff.

'Provision should be made by the Provincial Councils for appropriate groupings of Authorities for the purpose of post-entry training.'

As will be seen, the measures contemplated for the several aspects of post-entry training listed are couched in general terms, indicated for the most part by the words 'guidance and adequate facilities', and are entrusted to the Provincial Councils or the local staff joint committees, according to the nature of the case. The *Survey* published by the Joint Council in 1950 contained some useful preliminary information as to the extent and manner in which this article of the Scheme had been implemented. On the whole, it revealed that the response of the Local Authorities had not been very full. Some Authorities had done practically nothing, and the same was true of some Provincial Councils. Allowance should, however, be made for two factors. First, both Provincial Councils and Local Authorities were occupied in the first few years after the inception of the National Scheme in applying other aspects of it, and particularly those relating to the classification and grading of staff. Secondly, universities and teaching institutions and colleges, as well as local education authorities themselves in respect of their responsibilities for further education, all had difficulties in restoring or developing facilities of a kind which can assist the Local Government Service, after the disorganization and deprivations of wartime. The way should now be clear for a concentration on this very important aspect of the National Scheme. One or two Provincial Councils have already made advances on a wide front which should be a great encouragement to others and show what can be done. The South Western Provincial Council, with the co-operation and help of a variety of teaching agencies in that part of the country, and particularly the University College of the south-west at Exeter and the University of Bristol, devised at a very early stage, and has since extensively applied, an admirable scheme which, if it does not bring facilities literally to the doorstep of staffs in the scattered communities of that area, certainly brings them to a large number of centres easily accessible to willing officers encouraged by a willing employer. The facilities organized by the four Provincial Councils in the metropolitan area are also excellent.

In July 1949 the National Joint Council supplemented the

provisions for post-entry training in a very important way. In another section of the Charter, i.e. that relating to conditions of service, provision was made for the payment of monetary grants for the passing of approved examinations. In reviewing the list of examinations to be recognized for such grants, the Local Government Examinations Board arrived at the conclusion that payment of grants for examination successes was not sound in principle, as the real reward of the successful examinee was his eligibility for promotion on the basis of his qualification when opportunity presented itself. It considered that the better course was to afford financial assistance towards studies appropriate to the work of the department in which the officer is employed, and put forward a scheme of assistance. This makes no provision for payment of premiums, professional society admission fees, and similar expenses; but extends grants of 75 per cent of the cost of tuition, registration, and exemption fees, travelling expenses for courses of study and examination, and expenses of securing practical training where this is a condition precedent to the entry of an examination; and reimburses the full examination entry fee at the first attempt. In addition, it calls upon Local Authorities to provide full facilities for students to borrow textbooks and extends grants of 50 per cent (not exceeding £5) towards the cost of textbooks when these are not available at public libraries or office libraries of the Local Authority itself. The National Joint Council endorsed this Scheme, and declared it the better alternative to the scheme of monetary grants, but provided that the original provisions for monetary examination grants should remain in force until a Local Authority chose the new alternative scheme. Recently both sides of the National Joint Council have agreed that the new scheme alone should operate in future.

In concluding this review of Part I, it is 'convenient to notice one or two features in the requirement for a Promotion Examination already mentioned. Its object was fairly clear: to impose post-entry study on the General Division officers, and thus improve the standard of those who passed to clerical duties of a higher order—a class from which the Service had in practice drawn most of the staff who rendered fairly responsible administrative assistance to chief officers and their principal assistants. The passing of the Examination conferred no title to transfer to any of the higher grades, whether clerical or administrative; but, on the other hand, conferred eligibility for selection to posts in the higher grades should vacancies arise.

Promotion Examinations, as devised by the Local Government Examinations Board, were held in 1948, 1949, and 1950; but in 1950 it was decided to abolish the existing Promotion Examination and to establish in its place a separate examination for promotion to the Clerical Grades and an Administrative Examination at Intermediate and Final levels for eligibility for the Administrative Grades.

Although we have sketched here the Charter provisions for training and qualification, as part of a conspectus of the Charter, the whole subject is so wide and complex, and the developments arising from the original Charter provision for a Promotion Examination so far-reaching, that we postpone a fuller survey and discussion to Part III of this book, devoted to the whole topic.

General Conditions of Service

Part II of the Charter laid down general conditions of service, and dealt in considerable detail with such matters as office hours, overtime, annual leave, special leave, leave for jury service, maternity leave for women officers, sickness payments, payment of removal expenses, payment of expenses of candidates appearing before a Local Authority for appointment, travelling and subsistence expenses, and allowances for the use of motor cars provided by the officer himself. The detail of these provisions has had to be adjusted and supplemented from time to time, but there is, in any event, not much point, from the more general standpoint from which this book is written, in reciting minutiae of this kind. We may note, however, that the normal working week of the Service is thirty-eight hours, and that lunchtime is not included in the computation of the thirty-eight hours, as it is in computing the working week of other public services which may appear, on the face of it, to work a longer normal working week. Overtime is only payable to subordinate staff, and then only up to a salary level of £490 per annum; extra time of less than one hour on any day does not rank for payment; and the rates are plain-time-rate up to ten hours reckonable overtime, and time-and-a-quarter beyond that. Annual leave is scaled partly according to age and partly according to rank, from twelve working days to twenty-one working days, in addition to statutory and general national holidays, officers above the level of about £760 per annum having leave fixed by the Local Authority. The scheme of sick pay allowances is scaled according to service, and ranges from one month's full pay and two months' half-pay, to six months' full pay and six months' half-pay, with appropriate safeguards.

Scales and Grading

Part III of the Charter, headed 'National Scales of Salaries', established a series of national scales and contains provisions as to their use and application. The figures now current, which are set out in Appendix A, differ from those which were originally agreed. These were increased in 1948 in a process of consolidating 'War Bonus' with basic salary, as the result of an award of the National Arbitration Tribunal, following a difference between the two Sides of the National Joint Council in the negotiations for consolidation, which award effected some minor improvements in the scales for the General and Clerical Divisions. Further adjustments were made by agreement in 1951. As already mentioned, the range of these scales, as applicable to administrative, professional, and technical officers, was raised to the level of £1,000 per annum, following upon the extension of the National Joint Council's jurisdiction to this higher limit.

As will be seen, the scales are in five groups, each related to one of the five categories or divisions into which the Scheme classifies the staffs within the National Joint Council's scope. In the preamble to these scales, these divisions are specified in the following terms:

'*General Division.* This division includes officers engaged on duties dealing with particular matters in accordance with well-defined instructions and regulations.

Clerical Division. This division includes officers performing duties of a clerical character, which, having regard to their character and responsibilities, merit those officers being classified higher than the General Division.

Higher Clerical Division. This division includes officers engaged as supervisors of large or important sections of clerical work or on more responsible individual work than that of the Clerical Division.

Miscellaneous Division. This division includes officers whose duties are not wholly clerical in character but are of a specialised nature. These officers will not normally be recruited as juniors by competitive examination.

Administrative, Professional and Technical Division

ADMINISTRATIVE. The duties appropriate to this class are those concerned with the formation of policy, improvement of organization, general administration of instructions of the employing authority and the control of departments, higher work in the legal, technical, accounting, and other departments; also subordinate officers engaged on professional or technical work of a minor character.

PROFESSIONAL AND TECHNICAL. Officers with legal, medical, scientific, accountancy, secretarial, or other qualification covered by a Professional Institute, including civil or mechanical engineers, surveyors, architects, etc.'

In this specification, the reader will no doubt recognize a broad foundation for uniformities of the kind which characterise a service. But there is much in this part of the Charter that he may not understand, and on which the text of the document itself will hardly enlighten him, unless he appreciates the approach behind it, and is informed of the processes adopted for the use of these scales to determine remuneration. He will search in vain for anything in the Charter itself which specifies the remuneration to be paid to a particular officer, or for a particular post, or class of post. In this respect he will think the Scheme an unusual one, in strong contrast with other schemes prescribing national conditions, such as those for the Civil Service, the Teachers, or the Police. Unusual the Scheme is—and here again the underlying cause is the extremely heterogeneous composition of the Local

Government Service. In some measure, the approach which the National Joint Council had to make was conditioned by the disparities and anomalies in the pay of local staffs, either as between one Local Authority and another, or as between one area of the country and another, before 1946. But the major factor, which precluded, and will continue to preclude, at any rate over a large portion of the field, any scheme which of itself fixes standards of remuneration for a particular job, is the extraordinary variation in duties and responsibility which may exist in different places for jobs similar in function. In other words, standard remuneration of jobs under a documentary scheme can only be based on uniformities of responsibility and duty. In the Local Government Service there is a portion of the field capable of some such treatment. Since the Charter, the National Joint Council has, in fact, supplemented it by schemes providing standardized gradings for certain classes of officer. For classes so dealt with, the National Joint Council, that is to say, has specified the particular one or more of the Charter scales on which they are to be remunerated, assigned, in some instances, according to stages of qualification and experience, with discretion to the authority to pay higher scales for additional responsibilities not deemed to be covered in the standard job. Up to 1950, schemes of this kind had been devised, not without great difficulty, for legal, engineering, financial, and architectural assistants; sanitary inspectors; social welfare officers; inspectors of weights and measures; education welfare officers; and qualified assistant librarians. The Council had also dealt with Superintendents and Matrons of Children's Homes by what in effect was a Supplementary Scheme, based on beddage. But over a large portion of the field, and perhaps the largest, the situation is otherwise; no uniformities for standard gradings in the Charter scales can be found. This is a direct consequence of the large differences in the kind and scale of organization which different Local Authorities must maintain, and this, in turn, is a direct consequence of the large differences in the size and range of functions of Local Authorities, and in the kinds of area administered.

The kind of approach, therefore, which was open to the National Joint Council in devising the Charter, the one which it in fact made, and the one which lies behind the specific provisions of the Charter, was on the following lines. It begins with the assumption, implicitly contemplated in the establishment of the National Joint Council, that up to the level of its jurisdiction staffs could, and ought, to be dealt with by a tier of scales, of a number and range which could, in a broad view of the levels of subordinate staff to be catered for, and the corresponding levels of remuneration, accommodate all layers of staff up to posts of higher responsibility at £1,000 a year or over. Enough had been done by Provincial Councils to reveal that the staffs within the National Joint Council's jurisdiction could be broadly grouped into the Divisions already specified.

The next step was to fix the level of a basic grade which the junior would enter on the prescribed standards. There, as will be seen, a scale related to age was fixed, working to a maximum which was no doubt conceived of as a living wage for those clerical and similar workers, who would not, unless they passed certain tests, or acquired certain qualifications, be eligible to pass higher as vacancies occurred. Coupled with the establishment of a basic grade was the establishment of separate scales for a miscellaneous class largely intended for a variety of non-manual workers, e.g. inspectors, superintendents, etc., recruited without educational tests; but these scales have since been expanded to cater more adequately for the variety of staff affected and are now embodied in what amounts to a complementary Charter; experience having shown that groups included in it, although they remain 'officers' and within the scope of the Council, require their own specific code in the prescription of much service-conditions detail.

Above the basic grade, and up to the Council's 'ceiling', the object was to provide a tier of scales, each progressing from a minimum to a maximum by annual increments, into one or other of which the Local Authority would fit its staff, according to the assessment made of the scale value of each post in the establishment above General Division.

In the first instance the grading is done by the Local Authority. Part V of the Charter, however, contains a paragraph conferring on an officer a personal right of appeal to the Provincial Council if he is dissatisfied with the Local Authority's decision, or its failure to come to a decision, on 'any question as to the rights of an officer under the Scheme', and it was agreed from the outset and it is now formally acknowledged in an annotation that this provision extends to 'any question relating to his grading under the salaryscales'.

The initial application of the Scheme entailed, therefore, a huge task for the Local Authorities in grading within the scales; and this was followed by a similarly extensive task for the Provincial Councils (comprising representatives of the Authorities and the staff organizations) in the determination of appeals—a task only just being completed in 1950, when these lines were written.

In that year attention was being directed to the question of the rights of appeal that continued when the circumstances which affected a grading originally accepted, or one determined on appeal, had changed. If there is a substantial change in the duties of a post it seems proper that a new right of appeal to the Provincial Council should arise if the situation is not met by the Authority to the officer's satisfaction. On the other hand, the Local Authorities are very much alive to the danger of according rights of appeal in one case which will automatically confer new rights of appeal in others. A change in one man's grading may or may not justify a claim for change in other gradings; and it is not easy to state the determining factors, and to reconcile the differing viewpoints of employers and staff, in the precise language that can ensure just and consistent practice. But the problem is receiving the closest scrutiny and a solution will be found.

The machinery and procedure for appeals on grading represented unquestionably a very great advance in Whitley practice; but it is difficult to see how anything less could have been accorded to the staffs when the conditions precluded any extensive resort to the evaluation of jobs, by the negotiating machine itself, in advance. The officer and his organizations are in truth given a large say in the settlement of grading; but they are not given the determining voice. And one effect of the appeals machinery has been to deal the death blow to nepotism and favouritism as influencing the advancement of individual officers. The employers' side of the Scottish National Joint Council has regrettably not provided in the Scottish Charter for similar rights of appeal and appeals machinery to those in the English; but it is understood that certain rights to submit representations on grading, for advice by the Council, are accorded to the constituent organizations of the staff side.

The scales themselves are characterized by their short term in each case. For some posts the life of the scale could be conclusively shown to be too short altogether and to afford inadequate prospects to officers with high qualifications and considerable responsibilty. Indeed so much has since been acknowledged by the National Council itself, in affording a run of two or even three scales in succession for some of the professional posts dealt with in its schemes of standard grading. Another dubious feature is the overlap between each scale in the ranges above General Division, the commencing point of one being one incremental step between the maximum of the other. But this effect is somewhat mitigated by a provision that if a promotion or a regrading carries a man into the next higher scale he shall not be paid less than his salary prior to the transfer, and by the general provision that promotion can take place before an officer has worked to the maximum of the scale applicable to his existing grade. Promotion to any higher grade is conditioned to the existence of a vacancy in that grade, except when an establishment is altered or added to.

The scales carry certain additions as 'London Weighting' for staffs in the London area, i.e. the Metropolitan Police area; the additions being graduated according to age.

Throughout all divisions and scales increments may be stopped for unsatisfactory service, and on the other hand additional increments may be awarded for special merit and ability. Annual Reports are to be made in prescribed form on all officers, in order that proper records may be available in assessing qualifications and fitness for promotion, though the Local Authority can waive this requirement above Grade V. Attached to the scale for the General Division is a requirement for special assessment reports at the ages of twenty-one and twenty-six. If that at twenty-one is unsatisfactory the services of the officers can be dispensed with (legally, of course, this can happen apart from such a circumstance; see Chapter V.) subject to an appeal to the Local Authorities Establishment Committee; and if that at twenty-six is unsatisfactory further progression in the scale can be withheld.

Conduct

Part IV of the Charter, dealing with official conduct, contains a provision for the disclosure of relationship to any member or senior officer of the Authority by all candidates for appointment (and vice-versa), a prohibition of canvassing, a requirement for the declaration and communication of interest in contracts, and a veto on improper divulgence of documents and proceedings in committee. Interspersed among these provisions are others mainly for the officers' benefit: one requiring employment and payment by the Authority direct, enjoining Local Authorities not to appoint any officer on terms which leave him to provide and pay staff himself; another precluding the disclosure of information about an officer's private affairs without his consent; and yet another enjoining Local Authorities to adopt the recommendation of the Royal Commission on Local Government, and the model Standing Order of the Ministry of Health, for the discussion in camera of questions affecting the appointment, promotion, dismissal, salary, conditions of service, or conduct of any person they employ.

A very important provision for domestic procedure and appeal in cases 'where it is proposed to relegate or dismiss an officer' though embodied in Part III of the Charter, might have been looked for in Part IV. We cite and discuss it, however, in the next Chapter.

Part IV closes with a 'Code of Conduct':

'The first duty of a Local Government officer is to give his undivided allegiance to the Authority employing him. With his private activities the Authority in general is not concerned, so

G

long as his conduct therein is not such as to bring discredit upon the Service in which he is an officer. For that conduct public service is entitled to demand the highest standard.

'The maxim laid down for a court of law, that it is of fundamental importance not only that justice should be done in it, but that it should manifestly and undoubtedly be seen to be done, applies with equal force to the Local Government officer. Public confidence in his integrity would be shaken were the least suspicion, however ill-founded, to arise that he could be in any way influenced by improper motives.

'From this it must follow that the Local Government officer, as a public servant, must not only be honest in fact, but must be beyond the reach of the suspicion of dishonesty.

'He is not to subordinate his duty to his private interests; or to put himself in a position where his duty and his private interests conflict. He should not make use of his official position to further those interests; but neither is he so to order his private affairs as to allow the suspicion to arise that a trust has been abused or a confidence betrayed.

'He should be courteous to all with whom his duties bring him in contact.

'The public expects from the Local Government officer a standard of integrity and conduct not only inflexible but fastidious. It is the duty of the Service to see that the expectation is fulfilled.'

This code was one adopted by N.A.L.G.O. and the Charter negotiators agree to embody it as it stood. It is, as a matter of fact, an abstract of some of the leading passages dealing with Civil Service ethics which appeared in the Report, dated 28th February 1928, of a Board of Enquiry appointed by the Prime Minister to investigate certain statements affecting Civil Servants which had been made in the course of the case *Ironmonger* v. *Dyne*.

Part V contains a provision that any questions concerning the interpretation of the Scheme shall be referred to the National Joint Council for determination, and the important paragraph for appeals to Provincial Councils already noted, its remaining clauses being transitional.

Enforceability

The Charter having been agreed on 30th January 1946, it then remained for the Local Authorities to adopt it and apply its provisions. On the whole the process of adoption was rapid, the vast majority of Local Authorities thus recognizing

the authority of the new National Joint Council established
with their agreement. When these lines are written in 1951 it
can be said that with the exception of a handful of small Local
Authorities relying upon part-time staff the Charter is in universal operation throughout the Local Government Service.

Are its standards of pay, and such standard service
conditions as are covenanted for in its provisions, enforceable
at law? Once adopted its effect can be to import conditions
into the individual contract of service between the officer
and the Authority. While it is no doubt good practice for a
Local Authority to incorporate its terms by reference to it
in making appointments, it would appear that under the
general law of contract the parties could in certain circumstances be deemed to have contracted with reference to its
terms even if this precaution had not been taken.

As a collective bargain produced by the National Joint
Council the Charter was not, of itself, enforceable at law,
agreements between employers and trade unions as to conditions of service having been declared unenforceable by the
Trade Union Acts. Its provisions, and, indeed, determinations under it, such as those on grading, could *become* enforceable in law through the operation of the Conditions of
Employment and National Arbitration Orders of 1940–44.
These Orders, made in wartime under Regulation 58 of the
Defence General Regulations, 1939, were kept in force
in the post-war years, their general object being to prevent
strikes and lock-outs until all the resources of conciliation had
been exhausted, and to provide machinery for arbitration
by a National Arbitration Tribunal.

They made two kinds of approach. Firstly, they provided
for a 'trade dispute' to be reported to the Minister, and
rendered a strike or lock-out illegal unless the dispute had
been reported at a prescribed interval beforehand. They
defined a 'trade dispute' as 'any dispute or difference between employers and workmen, or between workmen and
workmen, connected with the employment or non-employ-
ment or the terms of employment, or with the conditions of
labour, of any person'. If the Minister were of opinion that
'suitable means exist for settling the dispute by virtue of

the provisions of any agreement to which the parties are organizations of employers and workers respectively', he could refer the matter under Section 2 (2) of the Order of 1940 for settlement in accordance with those provisions. Where, in the Minister's opinion, such 'suitable means' did not exist he could take any steps which seemed to him expedient to provide a settlement of the dispute. In either case, he could refer the dispute to the National Arbitration Tribunal.

The Minister could refer a dispute to a domestic machine such as a Whitley Council for settlement if he considered that it provided 'suitable means' within the meaning of the Order for dealing with the dispute. The Minister did in fact recognize the National Joint Council as providing 'suitable means'.

Awards of the National Arbitration Tribunal became implied terms of the contract of service, enforceable by civil process; and so also did determinations made by any agencies to which a reference was made under Article 2 (2). An enforceable award could in this way be made through the very domestic machinery through which the Charter was agreed, i.e. the National Joint Council itself.

The second approach made by the Orders was to provide suitable procedure for the observance of recognized terms and conditions of employment which had been 'established' in a particular sphere following upon their settlement by machinery of negotiation or arbitration 'to which the parties are organizations of employers and trade unions representative respectively of substantial proportions of the employers and workers engaged'. The Orders provided that such recognized terms and conditions shall be observed by all employers, and that any question arising as to their observance could be reported to the Minister by any organization of employers or any trade union which habitually took part in the settlement of conditions in the particular sphere concerned, in which event the order provided that the question should be dealt with as though it were a trade dispute. The alternative procedures already mentioned would then apply, and a decision of the National Arbitration

Tribunal, or of an agency recognized as 'suitable means', would likewise become enforceable in law.

As early as 1942, before the Charter was agreed, N.A.L.G.O. had taken a case to the House of Lords which established that Local Government officers were 'workmen' within the meaning of the Orders (*N.A.L.G.O.* v. *Bolton Corporation*, 1942). The provisions of the Charter, and the functions of the National Joint Council under it, were thus buttressed by the provisions of the Orders. After a reasonable interval N.A.L.G.O. reported failures to implement the Charter, or determinations under it, as trade 'disputes' or 'questions'. These were duly dealt with by the Tribunal, or by the National Joint Council itself on reference from the Minister, and very soon indeed the Charter became stamped with the character of 'recognized terms and conditions'. In 1951, the National Arbitration Orders were replaced by the Industrial Disputes Order, and the National Arbitration Tribunal by the Industrial Disputes Tribunal. The new Order did not include those provisions in the revoked Orders which had prohibited strikes and lock-outs. Otherwise its aim and effects were essentially the same. It continued to provide for the reporting of 'trade disputes', and of issues as to the observance of 'recognized terms and conditions' for settlement by an arbitration tribunal if not settled by suitable (domestic) machinery of negotiation and arbitration; and for awards of the Tribunal to be incorporated into the contract of service. It effected some changes in the conditions on which resort could be had to the Minister and the Tribunal; but these made no difference to the enforceability of the Charter; and what N.A.L.G.O. had done under the old Orders it could and can do under the new one.

The Scottish Charter

The Scottish Charter—to which similar considerations applied—is likewise operative throughout the Scottish section of the Service. It has some differential features. The provisions for post-entry training are not so comprehensive, there is power to prescribe a promotion examination, but none has yet been prescribed, and, as already mentioned, there is no provision for personal appeals by officers on grading. In addition, the scales themselves are cast on rather different lines. Originally, the General Division scale was differentiated for four groupings of Local Authorities of different size. These groupings are now, however, in process of elimination, and in 1951 the rates in the three lower scales will be assimilated to those in the highest.

The Agreements for Chief Officers

The agreements reached by the two negotiating committees for Clerks and chief officers are much more limited in their scope than the Charter, the initial purpose here having been the establishment of salary scales. As regards salaries (see Appendices B and C) both agreements made a similar approach. They recognize, and in fact recite, the difficulties of achieving complete uniformity owing to the varying functions of different types of Local Authority and the variety of local conditions. Any attempt to provide uniform scales for different types of Local Authority was abandoned. The scales are in fact founded primarily upon population levels, irrespective of the Authority's status. To meet the variety of conditions referred to, however, there is attached to each of the population ranges a range, rather than a particular scale, of salaries. Each salary range enables the Local Authority to select, for any of the officers to which the agreements apply, a particular scale within the minimum and maximum of the salary range related to the Authority's population level, so long as such scale as may in fact be chosen has the uniform span of incremental steps specified in the agreement. The Local Authority is thus enabled at its discretion to choose a particular scale within the appropriate range, in the light of differential local factors, and to pay some regard to personal factors such as the length of service of a particular officer. The prescription of ranges rather than particular scales also affords each Local Authority some elasticity in determining the particular salary relationship which shall obtain as between the specified chief officers, i.e. the Treasurer, the Engineer, the Chief Education Officer, and the County or City Architect.

One differential feature in the two agreements was the fact that the Clerks are given certain rights to fees for ancillary appointments, above the remuneration secured by the scales, which the remaining officers are not given. The differences in the two sets of salary levels will thus be increased in many Authorities, and the total remuneration of Clerks be higher than is secured by the scales themselves.

The agreement for Town Clerks and Clerks of District Councils provides that the Clerk shall be the chief executive and administrative officer of the Council and that he shall be responsible for co-ordinating the whole of the work of the Council. The definition of the Clerk as chief executive and administrative officer caused some concern to the other chief officers represented on Committee B. They felt that the Clerk could rightly be described as chief administrative officer and accorded the co-ordinating function, but that to describe him also as chief executive officer was to create doubt and uncertainty about their own executive responsibilities for their departments. A solution was found by providing in the agreement arrived at in Committee B that chief officers other than the Clerk should each be 'the executive and administrative head of the department and responsible therefore to the council through the appropriate committees'. It may be doubted whether the two definitions taken together really import anything new into the relationships which in practice prevail; or whether in fact they will be found to contribute anything to the removal of difficulties of the kind which occasionally arise, and which Committee A appears to have had in mind in agreeing to designate the Clerk as it did.

The agreements provide no formal machinery for appeals by the officer in the application of their provisions by the Local Authorities; but each agreement contains a clause declaring that each committee will be willing to 'act as a committee of enquiry and submit advice to Local Authorities in any case of difficulty between the authority and the chief officer which is submitted to them on the joint agreement of the parties'.

The agreements reached in Committees A and B met with
some resistance at the outset; and although, by the end of
1951, many if not most Local Authorities had applied them,
some were refusing to do so. In October of that year, the
South Shields Corporation obtained an injunction from a
Divisional Court of the King's Bench restraining the new
Tribunal from dealing with a 'dispute' (reported and referred under the terms of the revoked Orders and standing
over to be dealt with under the provisions of the new Order)
arising out of the Corporation's refusal to apply the Committee A recommendations to its Town Clerk; the dispute
having been reported at the instance of the Society of Town
Clerks on behalf of the Town Clerk as one of its members.
The court's judgment in granting an injunction (*Rex* v. *The
National Arbitration Tribunal and another, Ex-parte the
Mayor, etc., of South Shields*) turned upon changes in the
wording of the new Order in defining a 'dispute' as 'any
dispute between an employer and workmen in the employment of that employer connected with the terms of employment or conditions of labour of any of those workmen'.
Negativing an argument based on S.1 of the Interpretation
Act 1889, the court held that these words required a 'dispute' to be 'a dispute between an employer and more than
one workman *in his employ*, though it may be that the dispute
originates with a single workman and the others only become
parties to the dispute in support of the member of their body'.

Disputes reported by N.A.L.G.O. being disputes between
the employer and a plurality of 'workmen' in their employ,
i.e. the local N.A.L.G.O. Branch, N.A.L.G.O.'s position in
regard to the Charter was not affected by the South Shields
case.   For the same reason, the case did not affect
N.A.L.G.O.'s position in regard to the implementation of
the Committee B recommendations. Indeed, soon after it,
N.A.L.G.O. secured a settlement by the Tribunal in a dispute between the Durham County Council and members of
the local N.A.L.G.O. Branch in their employ, arising from
the County Council's failure to apply Committee B recommendations to the specified chief officers in its employ.

CHAPTER V

Constitutional Status

THE PRECEDING chapters will have made it evident that the advent of Whitleyism has effected considerable changes in the relationship of the Local Government officer to his employing authority. Whitleyism has not affected the Local Authority's rights, as an employer, or as a statutory body working under statutory prescription, to decide what staff it shall engage, or what officers it shall appoint or promote to particular positions; but unquestionably goes to the length of saying what conditions shall apply when staff are appointed, and (within limits) of determining, or providing for the determination of, their remuneration. To put it another way, the officer's contract of service with his individual employing Authority remains, but Whitleyism does much to determine what kind of contract that shall be, as between employer and employee, and in effect imports into each officer's contract of service certain elements not formulated by the contracting parties individually. In effect, the contracting parties contract on the footing of certain recognized conditions.

Manifestly, then, Whitleyism has curtailed—as indeed collective bargaining and Whitleyism must do in any sphere of employment—the employer's power and discretion in regard to the conditions of service of his employees. What we are most anxious, however, for the reader, and particularly the foreign reader, to appreciate in approaching the topics discussed in the present chapter is that Whitleyism is concerned with only one aspect of the relationship between Local Authorities and their officers, i.e. that of employer and employee in respect of the terms and conditions of their contract of service. The items and conditions of the contract of service being thus regulated by Whitleyism, the relationship of the Local Authority and its officer remains that of master and servant; and nothing in Whitleyism has affected the constitutional relationship between the officer and the elected Council in the discharge of Local Government responsibilities, the essence of this relationship being, in broad and general terms, that the Local Government officer is at the order and disposition of the elected Council which he serves.

In putting forward, in the introduction to this work, a conception of Local Government founded on political principle accepted in Great Britain, we said that it called for a full measure of responsibility on the part of elected representatives, and that this principle in turn required that elected Councils should exercise a full authority over their officers. We must look, therefore, at the relationship between the officers and their employing Councils in the light of this requirement in order to see in what ways and to what extent it is met in the British system.

The Relationship of Master and Servant

We have already said in general terms that the officers are in the relationship of servant to master in the eyes of the law, and remain under the order and disposition of their employing Councils. This relationship is in fact rooted in the system itself, as established by statute. In the British system of Local Government the elected Council is politically and legally responsible for the exercise of the local powers, and for the acts of its own agencies, i.e. its committees and its officers. In other words, the officer has no powers of his own which he may exercise as against the elected Council, or for which he is responsible to any other administrative agency than the Council. We are speaking in administrative terms, and disregarding considerations which may arise from another standpoint, i.e. the officer's accountability, in law, for acts which may affect third parties. We also disregard some exceptional arrangements for wartime emergency services in which Central Authorities have made use of the services of Local Government officers and in some instances exercised a measure of direct control over them.

Certain Local Government statutes, it is true, speak

directly to particular officers and make them responsible
for some particular duty. But the range of such prescriptions
is really very small. The duties so dealt with are of a
ministerial character, necessary either to keep constitutional
machinery working or to enable the Local Authority
actually to discharge the responsibilities given to it. One
substantial departure from the general arrangement must,
however, be mentioned. In the case of *Attorney-General* v.
De Winton, the judiciary took the view that a Local
Authority's Treasurer stood in a fiduciary capacity to the
ratepayers at large and could not plead the instructions of
his Council in justification of illegal payments. There may
be much virtue in an exception of this kind.

It should also be mentioned that in delivering judgment
in an appeal against a District Auditor's surcharge in 1944
the Lord Chief Justice is reported to have said that a Town
Clerk 'may be said to stand between the Council and the
ratepayers. He is there to assist by his advice and action the
conduct of public affairs in the Borough, and if there is a
disposition on the part of the Council to ride roughshod over
his opinions the question must at once arise as to whether it is
not his duty to forthwith resign his office, or at any rate to do
what he thinks right and await the consequences. This is
not so dangerous a course as it may seem. The integrity of the
administration of public affairs is such that publicity may
safely be relied upon to secure protection for anyone in the
position in which the Town Clerk was said to have been
placed'. Without criticizing or indeed commenting upon
the judgment on the particular issues in the appeal the author
would submit, with respect, that few Town Clerks had previously thought of acting on such a conception of their office,
and that it is difficult to see any warrant for the view that
the Town Clerk stands between the Council and the ratepayers, at any rate in any way comparable with the position
of the Treasurer. As to any moral duty to resign in the
circumstances cited, a Town Clerk is surely not to be
conceived of as one of the old school of amateur politicians,
but as a servant who owes his duty to the Council and the
Council alone. What publicity could be relied upon, and

what it could do to secure justice, seem to be debateable questions in view of the Town Clerk's tenure of office under the general legislative provisions to be mentioned in a moment or two.

The full significance of the statement that in the British system of Local Government the elected Council is responsible for the exercise of the local powers, and for the acts of its own agents, may escape the reader unless the position is explained a little more fully. As in other spheres, the realization of the ends which an organization or an institution exists to serve involves two processes—the formulation of policy and the execution of it. The cardinal feature of the British system of Local Government is that the elected Council is made responsible for both phases of action. The primary rôle of the officer is to be the executant of policy, but the system does not give him even in this sphere an independent responsibility. The Local Authority may, and in fact does, allot him responsibility in that sphere—a responsibility to itself—and one which usually rests, moreover, even as a matter of internal arrangement, very much more upon informal recognition than upon any formal definitions in lists of duties or such-like documents.

This situation, which has in fact made possible the growth of 'the committee system', is a characteristic of British Local Government. The arrangement is far from being a universal one, and is, in fact, in strong contrast with an alternative arrangement which obtains in most systems of Local Government outside the British Commonwealth. The characteristic of these other systems is that a definite responsibility for executive and administrative functions is assigned to a special agency in the Local Authority's constitution. This agency may take several forms. In America, it is the city manager (wherever the city manager system is there in vogue). In Ireland, the arrangement is similar, the city or county manager being given, in fact, all powers legally possessed by the Council, except those in a reserved list which are defined as matters of policy requiring the Council's decision or consent. In some continental countries, the executive agent is the Burgomaster. In others, including some Scandinavian countries, the agent is a small group, called the magistraat, which may be partly comprised of members of the elected body, exercising powers jointly with a director of administration. In Holland, a body similar in kind to the Scandinavian magistraat is the executive and administrative agent, and comprises several members of the Council together with the Burgomaster, the Burgomaster having in addition powers of his own in the maintenance of 'law and order'. In all these arrangements it will be observed that, either singly or jointly with others, a person who is, in effect, a paid official, is exercising independent powers in executive work and administration.

If certain conditions are observed, arrangements of this kind are not necessarily undemocratic, though English political thought would contend that they hardly permit of that degree of education of the lay Councillor made possible by his closer contact with the administrative process in our Committee system. In some Continental systems the Burgomaster has a responsibility to the State for certain duties, and at various times and various places has tended to become, in effect, an out-posted agent of the State machine.

The instances in which Local Government officers in Britain owe a duty to a Central Authority are such as involve functions of a ministerial character and not, as in many of the continental systems, questions of policy. Thus, Clerks of County Councils, and certain Town Clerks, act as registration officers for the preparation of the electoral register, and are acting returning officers in parliamentary elections. Similarly, Medical Officers of Health have a duty to submit certain returns and reports to the Ministry of Health.

In general, the control of the Local Authorities over their officers extends to their appointment and dismissal, in the sense that the Local Authorities are free from central control in these respects. There are, however, some important exceptions for particular offices which we shall notice later.

Tenure of Office

When the Local Authority is free of the central controls operative exceptionally for particular offices, the position is one of uniformity and the officer's tenure of his office is governed by Section 106 of the Local Government Act of 1933, which provides that he 'shall hold office during the pleasure of the Council'. This means literally what it says, and the Local Authority may put an end to the appointment whenever it so decides, irrespective of the grounds for its action. Indeed, it is not called upon to declare the grounds on which it may take such a decision, or to give any reason at all to the officer for the termination of his appointment. The words of the statute are so absolute that it was decided in *Brown* v. *Dagenham* in 1935 that the officer could not avail himself of a provision in his contract of service for certain notice to be given, when the Local Authority were in fact not giving that notice. In other words, a contractual provision for notice could not withstand the absolute force of the statutory words. Following upon this definition of the legal position, effected by *Brown* v. *Dagenham*, there was a general recognition that whatever might be said for or against a greater measure of security of tenure for Local Government officers for whose dismissal ministerial consent was not requisite, the existing statutory provision was unfair to the officer, depriving him of the right to such notice as might be contracted for. The National Association of Local Government Officers made representations to the Ministry of Health, and it was agreed that an opportunity should be taken to modify the existing statutory provision when opportunity presented itself. This opportunity was taken by the Government when it promoted the consolidating Local Government Act of 1933; and Section 121 of this Act contains a provision that, 'notwithstanding the general provision in that Act, or any provision in any other enactment, that a person holding any office should hold the office during the pleasure of the Local Authority, there may be included in the terms on which he holds the office a provision that the appointment shall not be terminated by either party without giving to the other party such reasonable notice as may be agreed'. The section also made valid provisions for notice in existing contracts of service, and made it clear that tenure of office at the pleasure of the Local Authority did not affect any right or obligation of the officer to retire by virtue of the provisions of enactments or schemes relating to superannuation allowances. In considering the effect of the section certain common law doctrines, however, must be borne in mind which it still does not override. The section makes valid the provisions for notice which before were invalid. It does not affect the right of the Local Authority under the law of master and servant to dismiss an officer summarily on any grounds which the common law recognizes as warranting summary dismissal, even in face of a contractual provision for notice. Here again, if a Local Authority, as master, were to exercise common law rights of summary dismissal, it is not bound to state the grounds on which it has acted, the test of its justification being the facts as found by the court if the officer brings proceedings for wrongful dismissal.

Special Central Controls

Let us turn now to note the exceptions. The salary of the Clerk of a County Council has to be approved by the appropriate Minister, and he may not be dismissed without the Minister's consent. This arrangement, made under the Local Government (Clerks) Act of 1931, represents a modification of the arrangement introduced when County Councils were set up by the Local Government Act of 1888. That Act provided that the Clerk of the County Council should *ex officio* be the Clerk of the Peace. Clerks of the Peace held office 'during good behaviour' and their appointments and salaries required the approval of the Secretary of State. These conditions therefore applied to the Clerk of the County Council. The Act of 1931 provided that the offices need no longer be combined, but imposed the conditions mentioned. Although, however, the dismissal of a Clerk of a County Council requires the appropriate Minister's approval, his appointment does not, although the salary must be approved. No similar conditions, whether of consent to salary, approval of appointment, or consent to dismissal, apply to Town Clerks.

The positions of Medical Officer of Health and Sanitary Inspector are also subject to measures of central regulation and control. In both cases, the essential qualifications are centrally prescribed. Until 1951, the appointments of Medical Officers of Health were subject to the approval of the Ministry of Health, where any part of the salary is paid out of the County fund, a requirement which brought in the County Medical Officer of Health, the Medical Officers of Districts and Boroughs electing to take a grant from the County, but not the Medical Officers of Boroughs or Districts not so electing, or the Medical Officers of County Boroughs. Somewhat similar conditions applied to Sanitary Inspectors. In 1951 control over the actual appointments was relaxed, but the Minister's approval is still required to the dismissal of either a full-time Medical Officer of Health (in whatever area) or a Senior Sanitary Inspector.

The office of Chief Financial Officer is free of central control; but in the case of the Surveyor, Section 17(ii) of the Ministry of Transport Act of 1919 provides that if the Local Authority elect to take a grant from the Minister as part of the salary (for duties as Road Surveyor) it shall be the term of the agreement that the Surveyor shall not be appointed or dismissed without the Minister's approval. In the case of dismissal, the effect of this provision is rather different from the effect of the statutory requirement for prior consent of the Minister. If the Local Authority dismisses a Surveyor, he himself has no remedy under the contractual arrangement effected under the section, since he is a stranger to the contract.

The office of Chief Constable is likewise subject to a measure of Home Office control. The pay and conditions are prescribed, and the Home Secretary's approval is also required to the appointment or to any dismissal.

The office of Chief Education Officer was formerly one which was entirely free of central control until the Education Act of 1944, which made it a statutory office, i.e. an appointment which a Local Education Authority had to make, and imposed the requirement that before making the appointment the Local Authority must consult the Minister and submit the 'short list' of selected candidates to him; also providing that 'if the Minister is of opinion that any person whose name is so submitted to him is not a fit person to be Chief Education Officer of the Authority he may give directions prohibiting his appointment'.

The Childrens' Act of 1948 contains a similar provision in relation to the appointment of Children's Officer. Neither Act requires the Minister's consent to dismissal. Inspectors of Weights and Measures and Inspectors of Gas Meters must hold certificates of qualification issued by the Board of Trade, but otherwise their appointments are free of central control.

The diversity of these controls reflects the piecemeal legislation which imposed them. Brought together, and looked at to-day, they present every appearance of inconsistency and anomaly. It is difficult to imagine any reason for the requirement of ministerial consent to the dismissal of the Clerk to the County Council which would not equally apply to the office of Town Clerk. Nor is it the fact, at any rate to-day, that, as the Hadow Committee suggested, these controls are for the most part confined to offices in services for which there is a direct Government grant. In so far as any of the controls are based on this consideration, it is difficult to see why the Chief Financial Officer should not be caught in the net. While minimum qualifications have been imposed in some instances, in others they have not. It is only to dismissal that the Minister's consent is required in some cases, while in others it is required to the appointment itself. And if one refers to parliamentary statements when the relevant legislation was passing through or before Parliament, the motives for these controls have also varied, the maintenance and efficiency of vital services being the uppermost motive in some instances, while in others it has been the protection of an office peculiarly exposed to attack by vested interests of one kind or another.

This situation makes it difficult to discuss the merits of the exceptions to the general rule without going into unwarrantable detail. It would be unfair not to recognize that the controls have often been of benefit to good Local Government. At a time when the Local Authorities' recruiting practice was not as orderly as it is to-day, or as free from

H

nepotism, or when they tended to undervalue recognized qualifications, the prescription of minimum qualifications and the requirement of consent to the actual appointment were often effective to procure the calibre of personnel which the Service demanded. If such prescriptions may have irritated the Local Authority with clean hands and knowledgeable judgment, they were a useful check on the backward Authorities. What merit provisions for ministerial consent to dismissal possess from an officer's standpoint, how far they may be due to officers in general, or to particular officers, as safeguards against arbitrary dismissal, we shall discuss later.

In what circumstances, if any, are central controls in this sphere justifiable at all on the principles on which British Local Government is supposed to rest? Sanction to appointment or dismissal appears wrong in principle, and so, in the main, the Local Authorities argue. The Central Government can argue in reply, that many services entrusted to Local Government are, in fact, national in character, and that the State must retain an obvious interest in the competency of the officers engaged. It might argue that even purely local services are entrusted to Local Authorities by Parliament, and that it is insufficient for Parliament to declare the obvious requirement for the employment of competent officers in statutory language unless there is some central administrative control which can ensure if necessary that the requirement is fulfilled.

In the author's view, the extent to which the controls can safely be discarded, and new ones obviated, will depend very largely upon the capacity of Local Government to order its own household; through codes of procedure accepted by both Authorities and their staffs, working in agreement to uphold standards and regulate differences. New factors are already entering into the situation through improved ethics on both sides in regard to all questions of appointment and qualification. Better standards and practice in recruitment, and in the ordering of relations between Authorities and officers, are coming into effect through the enhanced prestige of and the advice tendered by the Whitley Councils. The result may be to bring about, if not an entire abolition of the controls, at any rate a limitation of them to what seem to be their most virtuous parts. There may be virtue, for example, in statutory prescription of the standards which Whitleyism itself evolves by agreement, so as to bring the recalcitrant Authority, or the delinquent one, in line with those whose practice is unexceptionable. There seems no objection in principle, for example, to the prescription of minimum qualifications for major offices of well-defined scope and character; such at any rate as relate to services in which the State is directly interested, or are essential to the functioning of the Local Authority from a constitutional standpoint. There seems no objection to the submission to the Ministry of the name of a proposed appointee, in order to prove the possession of such minimum qualifications, or to certify that the proper procedure has been followed. What does seem to go beyond the limits of proper central control, at any rate in a system of Local Government which may be deemed to have passed its tutelary stage, is the assessment of competing applicants by the Minister, or, what may be very near to it, the disapproval of a Local Authority's choice on the ground that they might have made a better one, for this in effect is to substitute the Minister's choice for the local authority's.

Security for the Officer

It is difficult to find any justification in political principle for those exceptions to the general rule which impose the requirement of ministerial consent to an officer's dismissal. But the whole question of tenure of office calls for some comment from the officer's standpoint. Dismissal from office in any sphere is always a drastic sanction which social conscience will consider to involve human rights as well as constitutional controls. It is one which is much more severe in its impact upon a Local Government officer than upon many other classes of employee. Although the benefits of superannuation, including the benefit of the employer's share of the contribution, are taken into account in relating the salaries of the Local Government employees to levels of remuneration in comparable spheres in the commercial world, dismissal entails the forfeiture of these rights, and may entail them at an advanced age. The officer is entitled to the return of his own contributions on dismissal if no offence of a fraudulent character is involved; and if he can secure employment with another Local Authority within a period of twelve months he may pay over these contributions to the new employing Authority and preserve his rights with them. But it is not easy for a dismissed officer to secure re-employment in the Service, even if the employers' action in dismissing him was arbitrary or harsh, and he has a reasonable defence, or much to say in mitigation. The conditions in which he may compete with others for a new job are such as to put him, practically speaking, under duty of disclosure; and, in any event, if he gets on to a short list, his standing with his previous or existing employer is sure to become known, and is often the subject of specific enquiry. Local Authorities fight shy of an officer known to have been in trouble, and they cannot be expected to sift the 'rights and wrongs' for themselves.

If the officer lacks any legal remedy for arbitrary dismissal, is there any other effective protection available to him? He can, of course, seek the aid of his trade union. The responsibility is then cast upon the union to see what legitimate defence there may be. It is not the policy of the unions to bolster up misconduct or downright inefficiency, though if efficiency be the issue the union will probably argue that, since the Local Authority took the responsibility in making the appointment, the officer should be given time to enable him to procure another appointment before any step towards dismissal is actually taken. In offences of a fraudulent character, union policy is, broadly speaking, not to interfere with steps taken to assert the public interest, whether in legal proceedings or otherwise. It must be said that there are few Local Authorities who deny the unions the right to make representations on behalf of officers 'in trouble', and the Charter, indeed, contains the following provision:

'Whenever it is proposed to relegate or dismiss an officer (except for a criminal offence for which he has been prosecuted and convicted) the employing Authority shall, upon formulating such a recommendation, inform the officer concerned by letter over the signature of the chief officer, stating the grounds for such proposed action.

'Upon receipt of such a communication, the officer concerned may appeal, either individually or through his association or trade union, to an appeals committee of the employing Authority and shall have the right of appearing before such committee (with or without a representative of his association or trade union).

'The report of such committee shall be submitted to the Authority who will thereupon decide whether to adhere to, alter or withdraw the previous recommendation.'

It should be noted that this provision does not confer right of appeal to a Provincial Council, and lays down, indeed, what is a purely domestic procedure. This is as far as Whitleyism has gone to deal with questions of this kind for officers within the jurisdiction of the National Joint Council. In the case of chief officers and others within the scope of the two 'negotiating committees', the negotiated agreements do not provide for any particular domestic procedure; but contain a general clause directed to the removal of difficulties, and it is understood that the committees are prepared to assume an advisory function in difficulties arising between a Local Authority and an officer within their province.

If measures of this kind are ineffectual, what sanctions do the unions possess? They may, of course, blacklist an authority whose conduct they consider to have been unjustifiable, but while this course, in its effect upon the Authority's endeavour to recruit a successor to the dismissed officer, or upon its subsequent recruitment generally, has a deterrent effect for the future, it does not help the officer victimised. Among manual workers, wrongful dismissals have frequently given rise to strikes, but it is doubtful whether Local Government officers would resort to sanctions of this kind unless the evil grew to great proportions. It was possible to make a dismissal the subject of a 'trade dispute' under the National Arbitration Order, but the case re Crowther established that the National Arbitration Tribunal had no power to compel a Local Authority to reinstate a dismissed officer. The new Industrial Arbitration Order now specifically precludes the new Tribunal from dealing with such cases. It is a principle of the common law that the remedies of specific performance are not available on a personal contract of service, and it is understandable that there should be hesitation in conferring powers to order reinstatement upon an Arbitration Tribunal in face of the common law principle applicable to personal contracts of service. Indeed, a part of the difficulty in seeking remedies for the present position, and in securing reasonable measures of protection for Local Government officers, in face of their precarious tenure of office in law, and the dire consequences of dismissal, resides in the very fact, which the staffs themselves would recognize, that there are many practical difficulties in enforcing the services of an officer upon a Local Authority, at any rate for more than a limited time. But such a position need not, and does not, detract from the cogency of the argument that, short of serious criminal offences, or offences of a fraudulent character, dismissal should not entail all the consequences that it does to-day.

In seeking what kind of approach is best suited to the situation, which in essence involves the reconciliation of proper control in the public interest and the human rights of the officer, it is relevant to enquire what the risks of arbitrary dismissal are, and what, in fact, is the extent of any evil arising out of the present position. The risks are considerable. Local Government officers, and some in particular, such as certain chief officers, necessarily carry out their work amid contending forces in the local public, and amid much play of personal and political feeling among the elected representatives on the local Council. Officers who have a proper sense of duty may not show themselves as amenable to powerful interests outside, or personalities inside, the council chamber as these may expect, and may be exposed to much antagonism. They may incur displeasure through resisting suggestions or ideas which they feel it their duty to oppose as contrary to the policy they are instructed to carry out. Officers zealous in the discharge of services which affect private interests may be thought to have dangerously progressive ideas. Officers who candidly give their advice on policies they think unsound may be accused, in other quarters, of rigid conservatism, or of subservience to old-fashioned ideas. The possibility of victimization in these circumstances can never be far absent.

Does it, in fact, occur? This is a very difficult question to answer. In the author's view, victimization of this kind is not widespread, but the number of cases in which chief officers suffer for many years from uncomfortable relations with their employing Councils through circumstances of the kind referred to is far in excess of the number of cases in which Councils push their sentiments to the point of dismissal. On the other hand, there are many cases in which victimization is alleged in which, on enquiry, the union has been satisfied that there has been some ground, at any rate, for the Local Authority's attitude, and that the officer's conduct has not been impeccable. The fact that unjust actions are not of great magnitude is hardly, however, a complete argument against measures designed to secure justice. The majority of citizens are not criminal; but this is hardly an argument against the need for a criminal law or for the restraint of crime. Another consideration is that officers may be unduly amenable to improper pressures if they feel that they are defenceless against them.

Although officers have their anxieties about the present situation, it should not be presumed that they would fly to the remedy of ministerial consent to dismissal. They appreciate the standpoint of the Local Authorities in this respect, and those arguments against a remedy of this kind which reside in political principle. The best remedy lies in the resources of Whitleyism to provide proper machinery for appeal. In other words, the Local Government world should be in a position to order its own household. It is to be hoped that the Local Authorities will explore this line, offering as it does the alternative of domestic procedures which do not entail an expansion of central controls.

But there also seems to be a case for providing powers to the Local Authorities which would enable them to place an officer on the retired list, with a modified pension—powers which do not exist as yet.

The recent provisions in Civil Service rôles for earlier retirement without entire loss of pension may offer some precedent along these lines which might, with the domestic procedures also suggested, dispose of the whole issue.

Civil Rights

As to the civil rights of Local Government officers, they are precluded by various statutory provisions from being members of Councils or joint committees or boards which stand in the relationship of their employers. Only in one case, however, are they precluded by law from membership of Parliament, i.e. if they are employed by a County Council. The reason for this exception is not clear. If an officer becomes a member of Parliament without having arrived at a prior understanding with his employing Authority he stands the risk of the Local Authority taking the view that his parliamentary duties are obviously incompatible with his duties as their employee, and justify the termination of his service. A number of Local Authorities have in suitable instances accorded unpaid leave for a period long enough to enable the officer to make up his mind as to which career he will permanently pursue; but it would be difficult to seek universality for such a rule, as obvious practical difficulties could arise for the local authority in relying for any appreciable time on 'substitution' rather than replacement for the carrying out of his duties.

As to participation in 'politics', nothing has been laid down either in law or any code so far evolved by agreement between employers and employees. The following must therefore be regarded as no more than a brief indication of prevailing sentiment and practice. Chief officers are expected not to participate actively in party politics. There is the same expectation in respect of officers of senior rank whose duties are associated with the formulation of local Authority policy and the direction of its execution; though some authorities make no objection if the activity is outside the area in which the officer is employed. Considerably more freedom is accorded to the lower ranks of the officer class, but although the freedom is almost complete in the case of manual workers, even in their area of employment, it is suggested that officers even in the lower ranks are unwise to participate openly in party politics in the area of their employing Councils.

A full account of the officer's constitutional status and relationship with his Authority would extend to the consideration of his rôle in the discharge of the Local Authority's functions and his relations with the elected personnel in the machinery of administration. Consideration of space must preclude such a study here; but the reader will find this aspect of the subject dealt with in most of the works on Local Government listed in the Bibliography.

PART TWO

———————

THE SHAPING AGENCIES

CHAPTER VI

The Organizations of Employers and Officers

THE PRECEDING part of this book will have made it plain that the main agency shaping the Local Government Service of to-day and to-morrow is the Whitley machine. Behind the Whitley machine, however, stand, on the one side, the Local Authorities and their organizations, and, on the other, the staffs and their organizations. Moreover, the individual Local Authority itself has still a vital rôle to play, not only in the direction of its own staff for the purposes of Local Government, but in the application of schemes and conditions agreed through the Whitley machine. We may say, then, that there are three kinds of agency shaping the Service from day to day: the organizations of employers and staffs, the Whitley machinery, and the individual Local Authorities themselves. In this and the two succeeding chapters, comprising Part II of this book, we survey each of these agencies in turn.

The Employers' Organizations

First, then, as to the organizations of employers, that is to say, the organizations of Local Authorities. In many European countries the Local Authorities have formed one comprehensive organization. The situation in Great Britain is very different. Not only do we find that separate organizations exist for England and Wales on the one hand and Scotland on the other. We find that both north and south of the border separate organizations exist for each class of Authority. This is a situation which many have deplored, but without discussing its merits or demerits, or canvassing the possibility of change, we can readily see how it has come about.

In the continental countries where one comprehensive organization exists, organization along these lines has undoubtedly been facilitated by the fact that all Local Authorities enjoy the same status in law, and have in theory the same powers; though size, population, and financial resources result, in practice, in considerable differences in the measure and manner in which these powers are made use of. In Great Britain, as we have seen, the Authorities are of varying competency, being comprised of different types, each with its specified endowment of functions. Powers are in fact distributed, not uniformly on an area basis, but according to status, and it is a further feature of the system that the areas themselves are very largely segregated as between Urban and Rural. As a consequence, while Local Authorities of all classes and sizes have, up to a point, a common interest in the defence and furtherance of Local Government, while they make common cause against policies or interests which they may deem inimical to the public interests with which they are entrusted, and while they recognize that there is a considerable field for common interest and study through organized means, the interests of the several classes of Authority are in many respects in conflict one with another. There is a natural conflict, for instance, between the Counties and the County Boroughs; since the latter are walled cities, so to speak, inside the county geographically but not administratively, and in the conditions of recent years they have been driven to encroach more and more upon the county areas by expansion of their own boundaries, with many repercussions upon county administration and finance. Similarly, there is a natural cleavage between the Counties, on the one hand, and the Boroughs and Districts on the other, arising out of their competing claims in matters of finance and the distribution of functions within the administrative county. And underlying this situation at every turn there are the differing outlooks of town and country, brought to friction point between Authorities lying along their frontiers. This is but a brief indication of a situation which enters into practically every major Local Government controversy of the day. It is given without any critical intent. It would, indeed, be a great mistake to regard these cleavages merely as examples of petty jealousy or mistaken notions of prestige. They go much deeper than that, and are in some measure inherent in any structure of Local Government founded upon the principles we have adopted in this country. They crop up at every turn in the varying developments of Local Government. To come closer to the specific theme of this book, they impeded for many years, as we saw in an earlier chapter, the establishment of the National Joint Council. Even to-day the settlement of employer representation on the Provincial Councils is no easy matter, because of the varying classes and sizes of Authority which have to be accommodated in the schemes of representation on which such Councils are founded.

Of course, the several associations do co-operate to a very great extent, and on many matters take joint action. In the end, they co-operated and took joint action in devising the new constitution for the National Joint Council, in order to eliminate difficulties of representation amongst the several types of Authority, and so re-establish the Council on a new and strengthened basis. They have since gone one step further and established a joint advisory committee to deal, from an employer's standpoint, with questions of policy relating to service conditions in all classes and grades of Local Authority employment. In this way, the employers now maintain a conspectus of service conditions, not only for Local Government officers, but for the teachers, the police, firemen, manual workers, and other sections, with a view to balance and proper relationship. No doubt the business arising in all the Whitley Councils with which Local Authorities are connected, and all direct negotiations with trade unions or similar organizations, are carefully watched, with an eye to the repercussions arising in one sphere from action proceeding, or agreements reached, in another. Such a development is natural and normal, and cannot seriously be objected to by the trade unions. The unions mature their own policies through their own organs of expression and government. They themselves often seek to realize the same objectives in several spheres of negotiation, as for example when N.A.L.G.O. pursues its service conditions policy, not only for Local Government staffs through the National Joint Council, but for those sections of its membership in the Electricity, Gas, Health, and Transport Services, through the appropriate Whitley bodies established in these fields. On the whole, it is good for the strength and stability of the Whitley machinery that a high degree of organization should be at work in the approach of both sides.

In England and Wales the organizations of Local Authorities are the County Councils Association, the Association of Municipal Corporations, the Urban District Councils Association, the Rural District Councils Association, and the Standing Joint Committee of Metropolitan Boroughs, the existence of the latter not precluding the Metropolitan Boroughs from also being members of the Association of Municipal Corporations. All these associations are represented on the employers' side of the National Joint Council and on the two negotiating committees for chief officers.

In Scotland the organizations are the Association of County Councils in Scotland, Convention of the Royal Burghs (now representing all the Burghs), and the Association of Counties of Cities, all participating in the Scottish Joint Council.

Professional Societies, etc.

Turning to the staff organizations, we notice first those having a membership belonging to a particular occupational grouping in the Service. We may shortly call them professional societies, though not all their members belong to professions in the older and usual sense of the term. Bearing in mind the occupational range of the Service, as indicated in an earlier chapter, the reader will not be surprised to learn that they are extremely numerous. It is also the fact that their status, objects, and activities vary very considerably. For these reasons we do not propose to enumerate them or to survey them in detail. It is necessary, however, to notice the broad types into which they can roughly be classified. Few of them are trade unions in the sense that they have become registered or certified as such under the Trade Union Acts; and although some of them interest themselves in the service conditions of their members not all of them play a major rôle in negotiation with employers. None of them are directly represented on the National Joint Council, though on Committees A and B the bulk of the representation on the staff side is from organizations representative of the groups of chief officers which these committees deal with.

The first category we shall distinguish is that of the purely professional institute, established as an examining body and conferring a recognized qualification. In this category come the Institute of Municipal Treasurers and the Institute of Municipal Engineers. Until fairly recently these bodies also took the service conditions of their members within their purview and undertook propaganda and, to some extent, negotiation, in furtherance of salary scales for their members which they had formulated unilaterally. Recently, however, the policy of the membership has changed to the extent of withdrawing the institutes from service conditions activities and forming new bodies, namely, the Association of Local Government Financial Officers and the Association of Municipal Engineers to deal with this aspect of their members' interests. It is representatives of these latter emanations in the two professions indicated which represent their respective groups on Committee B.

Similar steps have been under consideration in a second category of professional organizations which exist to promote professional or occupational study, and some of which confer a qualification, but which are continuing, at any rate for the time being, to interest themselves in service conditions, e.g. the Sanitary Inspectors' Association and the Rating and Valuation Officers' Association.

Thirdly, there is a group of associations which, although they have not established a qualification, genuinely interest themselves in studies appropriate to their particular functions in the Service. The Society of Town Clerks is to be counted in this third group. It confers no qualification of its own, for most of its members are solicitors, and most of these in turn are members of the Law Society, the body which governs the solicitors' branch of the legal profession.

A few associations in yet a fourth category exist mainly to see that the interests of the occupational groups they represent are duly taken into account by those who play the major rôle in negotiation with the employers.

I

To the extent that any of these group organizations in the Service are purely professional, they are mostly self-governing in respect of the qualifications they confer. But the trade union for Local Government officers in general, namely N.A.L.G.O., maintains a keen interest in their activities; many of them make use of N.A.L.G.O.'s education institute; and indeed some of them entirely rely upon it for tuition in correspondence courses.

In so far as these bodies concern themselves with service conditions and salaries, how do they function, since none of them are directly represented on the National Joint Council? The answer is that, with some exceptions for the organizations of chief officers, they work through N.A.L.G.O., being formally linked with it.

N.A.L.G.O. itself, however, is not built up by representation of occupational groupings. Its electorate, as we shall see, is its membership at large, divided into suitable geographical units or units with a common employer, for the purposes of its representative structure at national, regional, and local levels. How, then, do the professional societies interesting themselves in service conditions work through N.A.L.G.O.? Collectively, they may join what is called its Joint Consultative Committee, which comprises representatives of the professional and sectional societies, acting as an advisory body to its National Council, its committees, and its negotiating staff. In addition, N.A.L.G.O. conducts activities which involve special group interests in direct consultation with the professional society concerned, as occasion arises.

The development of Whitley machinery, and the exigencies of day-to-day work and negotiation through it, have orientated the contacts between N.A.L.G.O. and the sectional societies more and more towards direct contacts at official levels as questions arise. Generally speaking, representations, arguments, claims, and information take their course in these days direct from the sectional society concerned to N.A.L.G.O.'s National Executive Council, its committees or its staff, as the case may require; and action proceeds in the negotiating field by reference from these

agencies of N.A.L.G.O. to the staffs' side of the National
Joint Council or other Whitley body concerned. The
National Joint Council itself has evolved the practice of
hearing representatives of sectional organizations in the
discussion of claims advanced by the staffs' side representatives on behalf of any particular group. It is too much to
hope that sectional aspirations will always be realized, and
the representatives of the major organization have obviously
no easy task in keeping a due balance between the various
groups of the Service. But the machine works.

Some of the chief officer organizations have no formal link
with N.A.L.G.O. such as we have described. The majority
of chief officers, however, are individual members of
N.A.L.G.O., and while in Negotiating Committees A and B
it is the chief officers' sectional organizations which supply
the representation on the staffs' side and thus assume
responsibility for the task of negotiation, N.A.L.G.O.'s
services are available to the members in the implementation
of agreed conditions as in other matters.

The National Association of Local Government Officers

Trade unionism for Local Government Officers virtually
commenced in 1905, with the formation in that year of the
National Association of Local Government Officers. It is
true that before that date, and even subsequently, a small
number of Local Government officers joined trade unions
catering mainly for manual workers, some of which had
established sections for clerical workers in the same sphere
of employment. But the vast body of hitherto unorganized
Local Government officers were eventually drawn into
N.A.L.G.O., and many who had initially joined the other
unions subsequently transferred their allegiance. To-day
some of these unions retain a comparatively small membership drawn from certain fringes of the officer class; and their
representatives and N.A.L.G.O.'s participate amicably in
the Whitley machinery.

The Association did not at first procure formal recognition
as a trade union, but from the very first its objects were those
of a trade union, and later on it took the formal steps under

the Trade Union Act of 1913 to procure the statutory recognition of its status and was certified as a Trade Union under the Act. It has not, like most of the manual workers' trade unions, and some trade unions of black-coats, affiliated to the Labour Party. Nor has it, again like most other trade unions, affiliated to the Trades Union Congress. Its policy has been, as an organization of public officers whose duty it is to serve employing Councils of varying political complexion and to be politically impartial in the discharge of duty, to hold aloof from any affiliation with, or commitments to, any political party. The question whether affiliation to the Trades Union Congress would carry any such implication has been the subject of some difference of opinion among its membership; but as matters stood in 1950, the Association had declared itself averse to affiliation after a majority vote against this course in a ballot of membership taken in the previous year. The verdict was unquestionably based on the view that, despite the absence of any constitutional link, the Trades Union Congress had a *de facto* association with the Labour Party, and that there was a particular association with the Labour Party through the participation of Congress in 'the National Council of Labour' along with the Co-operative Party and the Labour Party itself.

But these circumstances do not mean that the Association is not a trade union. Still less do they mean that the Association does not subscribe to the principles of trade unionism. They have not, in fact, precluded the Association from establishing joint machinery with both the Trades Union Congress and other organizations interested in the Local Government field for consultation in matters of mutual concern; or from operating, under the auspices of the Trades Union Congress and in agreement with other unions, certain regulative principles approved by Congress for the establishment of orderly inter-union relationships in recruitment, and for the avoidance of demarcation disputes. It may also be said, without reflection on other unions, that N.A.L.G.O.'s trade-union policy has been shaped to the conception of a relationship with its employers rather different from that of unions which for the most part have dealt with manual workers in private employment. Negatively, the Association has felt that moral if not legal limitations upon extreme sanctions such as strike action, bear more strongly upon unions of staffs in the public services than upon other unions. Positively, it has, with a similar sense of what is due to the public, deliberately sought a wide sphere for collaboration with its employers, not only in the establishment and use of conciliatory machinery and procedures, but in the development and prescription of standards of training and efficiency. Indeed, what we are anxious to emphasise in drawing these distinctions, without reflection upon the policy of other organizations, are the consequencies which have followed from the formation of a union of Local Government officers with a positive policy of co-operating with the employers in large sectors of common interest. What has, in fact, followed, has been the establishment of a Service in the sense in which we have defined it, built upon established national service conditions, supported by trade-union organization and activity, and also upon standards of conduct, qualification and efficiency arrived at through a process of collaboration and agreement with the employers.

The National Association of Local Government Officers has a membership, according to the return for 1950, of about 209,000. This figure gives it the sixth place in size among all trade unions in Great Britain, and the first place in Great Britain among all organizations of black-coated workers. There is every reason to believe, indeed, that the Association is the largest organization of black-coated workers in the world. There is certainly no organization of black-coated workers in Europe which in any way approaches the size mentioned, and even in the United States of America none of the black-coated organizations have attained a figure of more than about 100,000.

Of the total membership for the year cited, about 150,000 members were in the Local Government Service. From the inauguration of the Association in 1905 until the year 1946 the membership was exclusively drawn from the Local Government Service. In 1945 the programme of nationalization announced by the Labour Government elected in that year made it clear that Local Authority gas and electricity undertakings, their hospitals, and possibly their passenger transport undertakings, would pass over, together with corresponding units privately owned, to new statutory agencies of nationalization. The staffs desired to remain in membership of the Association, and indeed it was at this crucial juncture that they most needed its services in the transfer to new employment for which new negotiating machinery would have to be built up. At the same time, the staffs in the units of private enterprise, most of whom had remained largely 'unorganized', were turning their thoughts towards trade-union membership; and from the Association's own point of view it would have been difficult to restrict its interest in the new fields to the portions of the staff transferred from Local Government after nationalization was effected. Accordingly, the Association decided to amend its rules to provide for the retention of the ex-Local Authority staffs and the recruitment of staffs in private employment in advance of nationalization in these fields. There were, of course, other bodies interested in the staffs still unorganized; and although the Association's membership in the four new fields mentioned is a substantial one, the Association has nothing like the predominant position here which it enjoys in its main and original field of Local Government.

The extent of the Association's membership in the field with which we are here concerned is, of course, a reflection of its comprehensive basis, extending to all classes and grades of Local Government officer, i.e. the whole of the administrative, professional, technical and clerical staffs, stopping short of the manual workers. There are, as we have seen, certain classes of Local Government officer who also belong to sectional bodies. There are some chief officers, who, although eligible, have not joined the Association. But taking the Service as a whole, the ratio of actual to potential membership is somewhere in the region of 90 per cent, and even the majority of chief officers are, in fact, in membership.

To have organized and steered an association founded upon this comprehensive principle of recruitment, and to have gathered in so high a proportion of the potential, by voluntary recruitment, represents a unique achievement in the field of trade unionism.

No other trade union in Great Britain has a similar composition. The trade unions catering for the Civil Service cater for specified layers. There is one organization for the administrative layer, one for the executive officers, one for the professional Civil Servants, one for the clerks, and so on. Even among the teachers, there are several trade unions, and not one. In most parts of the Continent, and in America, the trade unions for public officers, and indeed for 'black-coats' generally, also cater for particular groups or layers.

The Association is also unique in one further feature of its activities, namely, the range of what may shortly be called its welfare services for its members, over and above the primary functions of trade-union protection (including legal protection). To its educational policy we have already made reference. It entails many external contacts with universities and professional bodies, direct participation in the important work now falling to the National Joint Council and its associated organ, the Local Government Examinations Board, and extends to the running of national summer schools at home and abroad and week-end schools on a provincial basis. The Association's own Correspondence Institute has still a wide field of work which has been kept adjusted to the changing pattern of education and qualifications in recent years. In all this educational work, the interest and effort of the ordinary member are enlisted. In each Branch there is an Education Correspondent, who not only assists the Branch in any educational activity with a local aspect, but acts as a channel of reference and help between the Association's Education Department at head-quarters and the ordinary member in the locality. In addition to the agencies at national and local levels, there is an Area Education Sub-Committee in each of the Association's regional areas, and these bodies are particularly valuable for contact with Provincial Councils and the universities in the application of the Charter provisions for education and training.

In its work of stimulating the interest of the citizen in

Local Government, expanding his knowledge of it, and co-operating with the Local Authorities in this necessary work, the Association's public relations activities have also an educative effect upon its membership. The reports of the Association's Reconstruction Committee on the Structure of Local Government, and on the Relations of the Local Authority to the Public and the Press, which won wide notice in 1945, are illustrations in point, as also is the travelling exhibition which the Association assembled in recent years, and which by co-operation with the Local Authorities must have been seen by hundreds of thousands of citizens in the course of an itinerary which extended to all parts of the country. In this aspect of its work, as in the sphere of education, the Association works through and is helped by Public Relations Correspondents in each Branch, and by the Public Relations Sub-Committee of its District Committees, working on much the same lines as the similar agencies for education.

The reader will probably not be surprised to learn that the Association has a substantial Benevolent and Orphan Fund, funds of this kind being fairly common among organizations of employees. Nor will he be surprised to learn that the Association maintains a convalescent home or runs a monthly journal. He might, however, be considerably surprised to learn that it also runs two holiday centres and a private hotel, the former offering special facilities for young families.

The most considerable enterprise established by the Association for the benefit and use of its members are, however, a Building Society, a Provident Society and an Insurance Society. The Building Society, which is incorporated under the Building Society Acts, though not to be compared with the giants of the commercial world, has grown to substantial size and its assets now total seven to eight million pounds. So, also, has the Insurance Society, named the National and Local Government Officers' Mutual Insurance Association, shortly called 'Logomia', and incorporated under the Industrial and Provident Societies Acts. It transacts Life, Household, Fire and Motor Car Insurance and Fidelity Guarantee, and its total assets amount to over a million and a half pounds. The Provident Society, incorporated under the Friendly Societies Acts, runs schemes for supplementary sick pay and hospital and nursing-home expenses, and has total funds amounting to over a million pounds. Participation in these societies is something apart from membership of the Association and rests on separate payments for the benefits contracted for. These three societies, referred to as 'ancillaries' of 'the parent Association', are run, as they must be, as separate legal entities, in accordance with the provisions of the relevant statutes. Their governing bodies, i.e. their Boards or Committees of Management, are representative of the members of the ancillaries themselves, but also include a proportion of members appointed by the Association's National Executive Council. There is a further link in that the ancillaries are served by the Association's staff.

The Association's policy is controlled by its Annual Conference, comprising in the main representatives of its 1,200 Branches. The continuous direction of its activities is, however, in the hands of a National Executive Council, which is endowed with the fullest executive power, subject only to the decisions of Conference on policy. As in other democratic organizations, the Council in practice assumes a wide initiative, putting forward proposals on policy to the Conference, though it has no exclusive right in this respect. Much of the work of Conference is devoted, not only to a review of the Council's work in the exercise of its executive responsibilities, as detailed in the Annual Report which it presents to Conference, but to consideration of the Council's proposals on policy, and of the additional and sometimes conflicting proposals which can be put forward by Branches, etc., through motions for the Conference agenda.

The Council includes the honorary officers of the Association, i.e. the President, Vice-Presidents, Trustees, Honorary Treasurer, and Honorary Solicitors for England, Wales and Scotland, respectively, all of whom are elected annually, and the Chairmen of the Boards or Management Committees of the Association's three statutory ancillaries; but in the main is comprised of members elected by ballot from the membership, in twelve electoral areas of regional character and scope. The Council works through a series of standing committees with a delegation of powers to the committees in some fields and a reservation of powers to the Council in others. The Standing Committees are the Service Conditions, General Purposes, Finance, Law and Parliamentary, Public Relations, Benevolent and Orphan Fund, and Special Activities, the latter dealing with a miscellany of welfare services including the holiday centres.

Between the national level of Conference and the Council, on the one hand, and the network of Branches on the other, the Association has an intermediate level of organization, through District Committees comprised of representatives of Branches in areas coinciding with the electoral areas for election to the Council. These District Committees have no executive powers in the sphere of administration, but they perform valuable functions in looking after the layout of Branches in their areas, in stimulating recruitment, and in supporting the national policies in the sphere of education and public relations through the sub-committees to which reference has already been made. In recent years, when negotiation has settled into Whitley channels, they have also given guidance to the staffs' sides of the Provincial Whitley Councils in the application of Whitley policy. The District Committees, moreover, have been useful forums for the discussion of policy at stages before formal motions from them or the Branches arise for discussion at Conference.

From a structural standpoint, the distinguishing feature of N.A.L.G.O.'s constitution is that it is unitary and not federal. Its governing organs do not reflect particular groups or grades of Local Government officers (or, since 1945, other groups of public officer); the principle of representation at Conference and on the National Executive Council being territorial and not functional.

In the circumstances operative since 1945 the Association's field of membership is now five-fold; and after a period of transitional arrangements, the Association is now adjusting its constitution to provide a proper place and status for the new groups of membership in the new fields, i.e. the electricity, gas, road passenger transport, and health services. Its unitary constitution and the existing character of Conference and the National Executive Council are, however, to be preserved. To give a proper part to the several groups of membership in the negotiation of their own service conditions, a series of sub-committees representative of the membership in each particular group is to be provided at the district level under the district committees, and a similar tier of sub-committees at the national level under the Council's main Service Conditions Committee. These new organs are to exercise certain delegated powers in the application of policy agreed by Conference, subject to the unifying direction of the National Executive Council. But the Association's constitutions will still make no provision for any kind of representation built up from different grades or occupation classes, and the changes are not therefore fundamental.

· The Association's constitution is one which places full control of policy in the hands of its members. What is more, it is one which is designed to bring its membership at all levels into active participation in its affairs, and work on its behalf. In its establishment, growth, and stability, and in the varied range of activity it carries on, it represents a great democratic achievement, for which the credit must go in the main to thousands of voluntary workers among its membership who have served it in the past, and whose active participation in successive generations it is the Association's policy to maintain. It is often said of trade unions in general that their ordinary members play little part in their governance. This cannot be said of N.A.L.G.O. Its membership is indeed of a kind which allows efficient service to be given by voluntary officers at all levels, drawn from the reservoir of varied capacity, experience, and qualification exemplified in the Local Government Service itself.

Its size and range, of course, have made necessary the appointment of a substantial paid staff. The Association's principal officer is its General Secretary, who is assisted by a standing deputy. The Association's headquarters is organized on a departmental principle with a group of departmental heads giving assistance to the General Secretary and his deputy, and assuming considerable responsibilities in the conduct of their particular sections of work. These departmental heads are the Chief Service Conditions Officer, the Legal Officer, the Financial Officer, the Public Relations Officer, the Insurance Officer, the Building Society Officer, and the Education Officer.

Extending as they do to a varied range of responsibilities in the very differing spheres of administration, organization, and negotiation, and to contacts with the work of Parliament, the State Departments, the universities, professional and teaching bodies, and other trade unions, the responsibilities of the higher staff are obviously on the highest scale, and call indeed for an unusual combination of talent and experience.

But the relationship of the Association's chief officers with the representative organs of government of the Association is very much the same as that of the Civil Servant or the Local Government officer himself to the representatives of the people. The officers do not control policy, though their advice on policy is listened to, called for, and not lightly disregarded, and they are, of course, given wide responsibility in the executive sphere. Being appointed by the National Executive Council, and responsible to it, their constitutional status is not quite the same as that of the officers of perhaps most other trade unions. It is N.A.L.G.O.'s National Executive Council which is answerable to Conference and not the officers direct. These arrangements do not bring the leading officers of the Association into the headlines when Conference proceedings are reported. Neither do they bring them into conflict with elements in Conference itself, as appears to happen in other organizations. The particular relationships which N.A.L.G.O. has evolved, as between its paid staff and itself, have many virtues; and they allow it to be said that here at any rate is an organization which is not in the hands of a bureaucracy, as trade unions are sometimes said to be.

CHAPTER VII

The Whitley Machinery

APART from the two joint negotiating committees for chief officers and officers with a salary level above £1,000 per annum, the Whitley machine for England and Wales comprises a National Joint Council and fifteen associated Provincial Councils operating in regional areas each comprising several geographical counties.

The National Joint Council and the Provincial Councils.

The National Joint Council consists of sixty members, thirty representing the employers and thirty representing the officers. The composition of the employers' side of the Council is twofold. Fifteen are appointed by the employers' sides of the Provincial Councils; each appointing one. Of the remaining fifteen, six are appointed by the Association of Municipal Corporations, five by the County Councils' Association, two by the Urban District Councils Association, one by the Metropolitan Boroughs Standing Joint Committee, and one by the Rural District Councils Association. The representation on the staffs' side likewise falls into two categories. Fifteen are appointed by staff sides of the Provincial Councils, each appointing one; and of the remaining fifteen, eight are appointed by the National Association of Local Government Officers, three by the National Union of General and Municipal Workers, two by the National Union of Public Employees, one by the Transport and General Workers' Union, and one by the Confederation of Health Service Employees. Owing to the preponderance of the National Association of Local Government Officers in trade union membership, the fifteen provincial staff side members are in fact drawn from that body. The members hold office from year to year, and there is provision that if any member is unable to attend a meeting of the Council or of any committee the appointing body may provide a substitute.

No resolution of the Council or of its committees is to be regarded as carried unless it has been approved by a majority of the members present on each side. It will be observed that this provision precludes any decision of an entirely one-sided character, but on the other hand affords scope for agreement through a vote contributed to by majorities on each side.

The constitution provides for the appointment of an independent chairman by the appropriate Ministry, holding office for a term of three years. The independent chairman is not given the right to vote. In his absence, a chairman is appointed from amongst the members of the Council, and as he will be drawn from one side or the other he retains his right to vote in the first instance, but is not given a casting vote.

The Council has power to appoint from its own members an executive committee and such other standing or special committees as may be considered necessary; but all such committees are to consist of an equal number of members drawn from each side of the Council. Committees may be given delegated powers; otherwise their proceedings are subject to the Council's approval, which may be given with or without modification. The Council has not attempted to divide its functions among a series of standing committees. In addition to one or two advisory committees on particular sections of the Service it appoints only one major standing committee: the executive committee. Much of the Council's work passes through the hands of this committee and it is, in fact, less of an executive committee than an advisory committee. It has been given no standing delegation of powers. It deals in the first instance with a large variety of questions that arise under policies and decisions already constituted; but also considers *ad hoc* references from the Council on many new issues which require detailed examination or a preliminary sifting of questions which the Council should determine. It has in recent years worked with the assistance of *ad hoc* sub-committees.

It is an established practice for each side to meet separately before the Joint Council Assemblies in order to review and discuss the agenda and to receive the advice of its officers. This practice has sometimes been criticized as opposed to the spirit of Whitleyism, residing, as this does, in a judicial approach free from preconceptions. On the other hand, it must be remembered that although the members of the Council are collectively empowered to arrive at binding bargains, each side must study questions which arise in the Council in the light of the general policy of their constituents; and the bearing of general policy upon specific questions often needs studied analysis. Neither side can hope to escape after-criticism; and a full opportunity to envisage the reaction of their constituents is due to both of them. At these separate side meetings beforehand, each side determines what line it will take at the joint meeting, or how far it will be prepared to go, or not to go, on any issue on which the other side may be expected to offer resistance. But this does not mean that debate is stifled in the Council itself. As a result of debate first views are often modified, and agreement or compromise reached. Failing that, debate often leaves a fresh impression upon one side or the other which brings agreement or compromise later on, after an interval of deferment.

The practice of holding side meetings beforehand is not extended to meetings of the executive committee, or indeed of any other committees or sub-committees set up from time to time. Both sides have so far taken the view that the committee level is one which should be left for a rather freer expression of individual viewpoints and for the fullest exchange of factual data.

The Council is empowered to appoint a secretary, treasurer, auditor, and such other officers or clerical assistants as may be decided. The Council has in fact adopted the practice of appointing joint secretaries, one appointed by the employer's side to be their secretary and the other appointed by the staffs' side to be theirs, both of them being appointed joint secretaries of the Joint Council.

In considering an arrangement of this kind, the inherent

difficulties of which will be obvious to anyone with administrative experience, one must bear in mind the nature of the task which the Joint Council has to carry out, its own two-sided composition, and the conditions in which Whitleyism has developed from the older procedures of *ad hoc* negotiation between employers and unions. The arrangement is one which, if not entirely uniform throughout the world of Whitleyism, is so prevalent in it that it can be said to be characteristic of the Whitley sphere. Whitleyism has been the product of organization of both employees and employers and the parties to collective bargaining do not lose their identity merely by agreeing to participate in standing machinery. Standing machinery requires joint secretarial service at officer level; and at the same time the parties continue to look for the kind of expert advice they would have received had they continued on the old lines of *ad hoc* consultation. It seems a natural development, then, for each side to have a secretary who can serve it, not only ministerially in the ordering of business passing through the Whitley machine, but as an adviser.

The virtues of this arrangement can be regarded as proven; but it is one not altogether free from difficulties of an administrative kind in the mechanics of the Joint Council's work. When the volume of business dealt with by joint machinery of this kind is considerable, a joint secretaryship in the full and literal sense of the term becomes, in fact, quite impracticable, particularly where, as is usually the case, the joint secretaries are located in different places. It is impossible for all correspondence to be double-handled. In pressure of work it is sometimes impossible indeed for even documents such as agendas and minutes to be a joint production in any full measure.

The problem has usually been solved by an arrangement, often quite tacit, under which the administrative work and the secretarial work of the Council as a Council is carried out by the employers' secretary. Agendas and minutes are prepared by him, after the utmost measure of consultation possible with the staffs' side secretary. The office work behind all this will be carried out by his staff. On the other hand, decisions of the Council usually go out under the joint names; and there are occasions on which the Council will call for a joint report, and even ask the secretaries to agree if possible on recommendations for the Council's consideration. All this, of course, does not preclude the staffs' side secretary, or the employers' secretary from briefing their respective sides; or submitting to one another representations which one side of the Council may desire to lay before the other. These are the general lines operating in the case of the National Joint Council.

They work well in practice, but it is not always possible to eliminate difficulties. The employers' secretary is exposed in that capacity to a correspondence with the employers' secretaries of fifteen Provincial Councils and the clerks of 1,500 Local Authorities. The staffs' side secretary is exposed in his capacity to correspondence with staffs' side secretaries of the Provincial Councils, the secretaries of numerous professional and sectional societies and professional institutes, and requests, representations and correspondence submitted by or through the staff organizations represented on the Whitley Council. It is not easy for either secretary to segregate all the correspondence which might ideally call for reference to the other. Nor is it always easy for either to judge what calls for joint action, or what may be dealt with by way of unilateral advice, explanation, or comment. It is no uncommon experience for a member of the staffs' side to complain that the employers' secretary has replied to a letter from the Clerk to his Local Authority in terms with which the staffs' side could not agree; for the staffs' side secretary to confess that he has no knowledge of it; but to be told by the employers' secretary that his reply represented his advice as employers' secretary to one of the employers' side's constituents, and that he had not thought any interpretation of the Joint Council's decisions to be involved. Similar complaints are raised by the employers as to action taken by the staffs' side secretary in replies to officers, branches, or members of the unions represented on the staffs' side. Circumstances of this kind are bound to arise from time to time, but any harm done is usually

K

capable of remedy through the resources of the machinery and the Charter; and when conditions precedent are so intrinsically difficult the machine can be said to function extremely well on the whole.

One variant to the device of joint secretaries, and one which has been adopted by one or two Provincial Councils, is for each side to appoint its separate secretaries, and for one of them—and tradition holds that it should be the employers' secretary—to be appointed as single secretary to the council as such. This arrangement has the virtue of creating one single channel for the Council's correspondence, and for fixing responsibility on one man, albeit he may also be the employers' secretary, in the discharge of purely ministerial functions for both sides. It carries the consequence, of course, that he has recognized responsibility for communicating anything to the staffs' side secretary which could be deemed of joint concern. But this rather more clear-cut arrangement could in certain circumstances place the staffs' side and their organizations at some disadvantage (and the secretary himself in a position of some embarrassment) in any major clashes of policy between the two sides, and in the interplay of negotiation, particularly if arbitration loomed on the horizon. It may have virtues at the provincial level which it would not possess at the national.

The work of the National Joint Council is financed through three separate accounts. Administrative expenses of the Council as a whole, other than the expenses of members in attending meetings and the salaries of staff, are defrayed from a common fund and borne equally by the respective sides. The employers' side apportions its share over the fifteen provincial councils' employers' sides, and they in turn apportion it among their constituent Authorities. The staffs' side apportions its share amongst the organizations represented on it. In addition, each side meets certain expenses of its own, and similarly apportions them. These include the expenses of members' attendance and the cost of its own secretariat. It is understood that the salaries of the employers' secretariat are defrayed by the Local Authority organizations, the staff serving other Whitley bodies in the sphere of Local Government. It is not unusual for the staffs' side secretary to Whitley bodies to be an officer of one of the organizations represented and for this organization to make no apportionment of salary and office expenses in respect of his services or those of any staff assisting him upon the other. This is, in fact, the arrangement operating in respect of the staffs' side secretariat of the National Joint Council, the secretary being the General Secretary of N.A.L.G.O., a small honorarium accorded by the staffs' side being paid into the Association's funds.

Turning now to the Provincial Councils, we find that there is a good deal of variation in the number of members. This is inevitable because the respective areas differ in size; and have a varying content of Local Authorities as regards number, size, and status. For these reasons, moreover, each Provincial Council has to have its own scheme of representation on the employers' side, and a variety of means has to be resorted to in the choice of representatives. Sometimes a ballot is held by the secretary. Sometimes the choice is made at a representative assembly of Local Authority representatives in the area. And sometimes appointments are made by regional committees or groups of the several Local Authority associations if such exist. The same difficulties of representation do not exist on the staffs' side. Accordingly it is not unusual to find that in many cases the staffs' side is considerably less in number than the employers. Decisions are subject to the same provision for a majority on each side as in the case of the National Council, and no difficulty arises, therefore, on this score. Following the usual Whitley practice where there is no independent chairman, the chair of the Provincial Councils is taken alternatively by the chairman of the employers' side and the chairman of the staffs' side.

The constitutions of the Provincial Councils are subject to the approval of the National Joint Council, and in the main they follow a model agreed when the National Joint Council was reconstituted. It has to be remembered, however, that many of the Provincial Councils were in existence for many years before the reconstitution of the National Council, and there are no doubt some points of difference among the provincial constitutions.

The Provincial Councils are given power to appoint standing committees, and at the request of the National Joint Council all of them have appointed appeals and disputes committees. These committees hear appeals under the Charter and can in this and other tasks be given a measure of delegated power. They often deal with or advise upon 'differences' of which the Provincial Council takes cognizance under Article 11 of the model constitution.

This article provides for conciliatory action by the Provincial Council in the event of differences between a Local Authority and its staff in the Provincial Council's area. The essence of the jurisdiction is advisory. In the event of any difference not being settled at the Provincial level it is to be referred to the National Council for decision. Similarly, a difference arising between the employers' and the officers' sides of the Provincial Council, is to be referred to the National Council for decision. The National Council's constitution contains no provision for settling differences between the two sides of that Council. The constitution of some Whitley Councils contains a provision for arbitration. In the existing state of the law, however, arbitration is in any event available by one procedure or another.

The duties of staffs' side secretaries of the Provincial Councils are assumed by the District Organization Officers of N.A.L.G.O. To find employers' side secretaries can be and sometimes is a matter of some difficulty. One or two of the larger Councils employ whole-time staff, or are served by the employers' national secretary with whole-time assistants in the area. But in most cases a whole-time appointment has hardly been justified in the past, or might not secure personnel of sufficient status. The situation has commonly been met by the appointment of some Local Authority Clerk in the area who has interested himself in the work, and whose Authority are prepared to let him act and be afforded assistance by his own office staff, with some appropriate recognition by way of honorarium. The growth of the work in recent years has, however, thrown some strain upon arrangements of this kind, and often causes the pace of the Provincial machine to be a little slow.

The Local Government Examinations Board

The Local Government Examinations Board is an emanation from the National Joint Council, being appointed by the National Joint Council. The immediate object for which it was established was to devise and manage the Promotions Examination to which we referred earlier on, and under its terms of reference it has in fact executive powers for the discharge of that function. By agreement in the National Joint Council at a later date, however, it was given a general advisory function to the National Joint Council on questions of education and training. In respect of these wider functions it is, however, purely advisory, and its recommendations are subject to adoption by the National Joint Council. It consists of a chairman appointed by the National Joint Council and about ten other members, some members of the National Joint Council and others drawn from university or other circles. The Joint Secretaries of the National Joint Council are ex-officio members, but the Board appoints a separate whole-time secretary. It also appoints an Examinations Committee which deals exclusively with examination arrangements and also acts as an expert advisory committee. Members of the committee need not be members of the Board, and the personnel of the committee is drawn almost exclusively from among 'experts' in university or administrative circles. The whole of the Board's expenses, including in this case the salaries of the secretariat, are borne in equal proportions by the two sides of the National Joint Council and apportioned upon their constituents in the same way as the Council's own expenditure.

The National Joint Council for Scotland

The National Joint Council for Scotland has a similar jurisdiction to that of its prototype in England, but it is an entirely independent body with no sub-structure of Provincial Councils. It has no independent chairman. The representation on the employers' side is apportioned among the Local Authorities' associations (named in the last chapter), and the staffs' side representation is drawn from N.A.L.G.O., the Clerical and Administrative Workers Union, the National Union of General and Municipal Workers, the National Union of Public Employees, and the Transport and General Workers Union.

Notwithstanding, however, that the membership of the National Association of Local Government Officers is now greater by far than that of the other organizations together, the scheme of representation on the staffs' side agreed at the inception of the Council has remained practically unaltered, and it gives the National Association of Local Government Officers only half the seats.

The Scottish Charter having made no provision for a promotion examination, no Local Government Examinations Board has yet come into existence in Scotland.

The Negotiating Committees for Chief Officers

Committee A, established for Clerks to Local Authorities other than Clerks to County Councils, was established in 1948. On the employers' side the representatives are appointed by the Local Authority associations, and on the employees' side the representatives are appointed by the Society of Town Clerks, the Urban District Council Clerks Association, and the Local Government Clerks Association (representing Clerks to Rural District Councils).

Negotiating Committee B has within its jurisdiction four specified classes of chief officer, namely, Financial Officers, Engineers and Surveyors, Chief Architects, Chief Education Officers, and the residual and general class embracing officers whose salaries are above the level of £1,000 per annum. The representation on the employers' side is drawn from the Local Authority associations and the representation on the staffs' side is drawn from the Association of Local Government Financial Officers, the

Association of Local Government Engineers, the Association of Education Officers, the City and County Architects Society, the Associate Section (which comprises Town Clerks' Deputies) of the Society of Town Clerks and the National Association of Local Government Officers.

CHAPTER VIII

The Local Authority as Employer

THE FUNCTION of the Whitley machinery in settling and applying a code of national conditions does not relieve the Local Authorities from wide responsibilities and a substantial volume of continuous work in the handling of their staffs.

The Task of the Authority

The salient features of the task which still remains theirs are fairly well visible. It is for them to decide upon the establishment required for their varied functions; and this involves, at every turn, not only the study of administrative and organizational requirements, but a review of the personnel required, in terms of qualifications, training, and experience, and the determination of their status, seniority, and grading. This task alone, affected as it so often is by the impact of new Legislation, by changes in Local Authority function, and by variations in the scope and volume of the work arising in this that or the other field of activity, is obviously one of a continuous character. Further work arises for the Authority in the actual making of appointments, whether by promotion, or after consideration of applications invited by public advertisement, involving the settlement of a short list of selected candidates, and the enquiries and interviews leading eventually to a choice. There are, moreover, some items in the national Charter which call for detailed administration by the Local Authority, e.g. the provisions for post-entry training, and others which involve adjudication in individual cases, e.g. discretionary extensions of sick-pay, the operation of the efficiency bars in the General Division, and the award of merit increments. And finally, cases of conduct and discipline may arise from time to time. This review of Local Authority tasks is not exhaustive, but it will go to show what a considerable volume of important work arises.

Machinery for Staffing

Whatever machinery and procedure the Local Authority may devise for dealing with tasks of this character, they should be such as gain the confidence of both the Local Authority and its staff. Both sides must be satisfied that they afford adequate time and study for staffing questions throughout the whole range of the Council's work, and ensure even-handed treatment for all the personnel concerned. The Authority should be satisfied that no differences are established in the treatment of personnel other than those which are founded upon proper considerations of responsibility, function, and qualification; and that its interests as an employer are being adequately watched and safeguarded. The staff should feel satisfied that no favouritism creeps in, either towards departments or individual officers. Of particular importance is it to ensure that staff grievances can be properly ventilated and considered and that the procedure for dealing with them is not dilatory.

If these requirements are analysed they will be found to call for a considerable degree of administrative integration. The Authority's tasks call for balance, proportion, and in many cases uniformity as among different sections or departments of the Authority's staff. There should be some agency capable of giving the Local Authority a comprehensive view of the body of paid personnel which it employs. There is the further consideration that to make visible provision, on whatever lines it may be, in the Council's administrative mechanisms and procedures for the handling of staff matters, is in itself a step which reassures the staff of their employers' interest in staffing matters and in the staff themselves.

Now, as is well known, the Local Authorities handle most of their work through a series of standing committees laid out on the 'functional' principle, i.e. there is a standing committee for each of the Council's main branches of activity or services, e.g. housing, education, highways, and parks. In the past, it was the practice for each of these standing committees to deal with any staffing questions arising in the course of its work, and to make its recommendations direct to the full Council. If, before the advent of Whitley schemes, the Local Authority had devised its own scheme of service conditions and scales of pay, etc., this would probably have been done by its Finance Committee, but the committees taking charge of particular services or departments were often left to handle the continuing application of the scheme in their respective spheres.

In theory the Council itself was expected to maintain a conspectus over the whole field of staff management, to apply any overriding controls, and to exercise the function of co-ordination, as and when recommendations came before it from one committee or another. In any but the smallest Authorities it is doubtful whether a Council can ever, of itself, exercise such functions in practice. At any rate, as the range of Local Government widened, many Local Authorities discovered that the usual committee arrangements were inadequate to serve their needs in staff matters, leading as they did to many anomalies in the views and practices of the various committees and to methods of handling staff matters which turned out to be as distasteful in the long run to the staffs as to the Local Authorities. It is not surprising, then, that even before the advent of Provincial or National Whitley codes many Local Authorities had taken the step of placing staffing matters in the hands of one central committee, mainly if not entirely.

Such a course was recommended by the Hadow Departmental Committee in 1934. The Departmental Committee thought that in the case of smaller Authorities the recommendation might be met by assigning the appropriate functions to either the Council's Finance Committee or its General Purposes Committee. For the larger Authorities, it recommended the establishment of a separate staff or establishment committee. The recommendation was welcomed by the staff organizations, and did in fact lead to a considerable extension of the practice of appointing separate establishment or staff committees. In 1945, in the negotiations for the Charter, the question was considered by the National Joint Council, and it was agreed to endorse the recommendation of the Hadow Committee. Accordingly, the preamble to the National Scheme of Conditions of Service contains a paragraph stating that 'It is desirable that questions affecting the recruitment, qualifications, training and promotion of officers should be assigned by each employing Authority to an establishment committee.'

The practice of establishing a separate committee is now almost universal among the larger Authorities; and even among the smaller ones, or among Authorities which have not seen fit to appoint a separate committee, it is common practice to assign appropriate functions to the Authority's Finance or General Purposes Committee; the committee selected often appointing a standing sub-committee to advise upon or deal with this aspect of its work.

From an administrative point of view there are certain limitations upon the creation of committees to deal with particular classes of work as distinct from particular services or fields of activity. (See the author's discussion of this question in his work *Municipal Administration*.) But it may be said that, with suitable safeguards to prevent administrative confusion, there are, at any rate, two such committees which can advantageously be established, i.e. a finance committee and a staff or establishment committee; and as a matter of fact it may now be regarded as standard practice for Local Authorities to include two such committees in their general layout of standing committees.

The Functions of the Staff Committee

It is not sufficient, however, for a staff committee merely to be appointed. It is essential to introduce at the outset, or to build up as quickly as possible by practice and if need be experiment, a carefully articulated relationship between the staff committee and the other standing committees controlling the various branches of the Authority's work. This may not be so easy as it looks, for certain aspects of the work are such as to excite the interest and even the direct attention of both the standing committees and the establishment committee. In other words, 'the appropriate functions' of a staff committee (to use the convenient phrase of the

Hadow Report) are not entirely, even if they are mainly, self-evident; and unless agreed and defined may admit of much administrative confusion, or at best entail cumbrous cross-references in procedure, and thus generate much friction with other committees and much discontent on the part of the staff.

In establishing a staff committee there is indeed always one broad preliminary question to consider. Shall every aspect of staff conditions and management be integrated under the staff committee, or are certain functions relating to staff properly left in the hands of the standing committees in charge of the services concerned? Let us cite some of the questions that arise. In the initial formulation of an establishment, should the staff committee proceed on reports directly made by the Departmental Heads, or should the 'service' committees be brought into the process by submitting recommendations after reports made by their own departmental heads? In proposals for regrading or additions to the establishment, should the departmental heads' proposals first be put to the service committees, or direct to the staff committee? To what extent, if any, should the staff committee be concerned with the actual choice of applicants for new posts, or with recommendations for promotions within the approved establishment? In the exercise of discretionary powers under the Whitley codes, or in the grant of superannuation benefits, should the staff committee consider all individual cases in the first instance? Or should the service committee handle them, and, if so, in which classes of case should the service committee be left to make a final decision, or to recommend the Council direct, or be required to pass its recommendation to the staff committee, with or without the need for final confirmation by the Council? In all these and many other questions, it may be taken for granted that, short of binding prescriptions settled by the Council, the service committees will consider that they are often better judges than the staff committee, since it is they who know most intimately the work of the departments and the departmental personnel, and can best appreciate some of the 'human questions' that can arise.

The author does not consider that any complete uniformity of practice is possible or desirable, but he tends strongly to the view that the aim should be to concentrate as much as possible in the hands of the staff committee, and to leave the departmental heads to report direct to that committee. There are, however, two aspects of the work in which he considers that functions can appropriately be left to the committee in charge of the service or department directly concerned, subject, of course, to any powers which the Council reserves to itself: firstly, the actual appointment of officers (other than any junior staff recruited on general lines) and the procedures preliminary thereto; and, secondly, dealings in the first instance with cases of discipline.

As regards the appointment of chief officers, he considers that the procedure need not be stereotyped in advance for rigid application to every vacancy that arises, but left to the Council's decision in each case, upon the assumption, which seems a fairly safe one, that the Council will itself take a particular interest in appointments at this level. It should, however, be open to the establishment committee, when putting forward the recommendations to the Council as to the terms and conditions of the appointment, to recommend the Council at the same time as to the particular way in which the applications should be considered and the final decision taken.

The foregoing view rests upon the assumption that a Council will rarely agree to give any committee powers of appointment at this level. Assuming, also, however, that the normal and proper procedure will be taken in regard to advertisement, short list, and interviews, there are many variations in the procedure for making a choice which can properly appeal to Councils as appropriate to a particular post, or to the Authority's own status, size, and functions. Many Councils insist on interviewing themselves candidates on a short list for a Town Clerkship; others will leave a general purposes committee to make a recommendation; and others a staff committee. Some Councils, again, would think that they could do no better than leave an education committee to recommend the appointment of a Chief Education Officer, and would definitely prefer a recommendation from that quarter than from a staff committee. But they might take a different kind of view if it came to the appointment of an Engineer and Surveyor, whose duties relate to the functions of several committees. And whether they would look to a staff committee for a recommendation in this case might depend on how that committee was composed, i.e. whether it was in whole or in part built up of the chairmen of standing committees, or whether (following the polar line of Local Authority thought in the constitution of finance and staff committees) the chairmen of standing committees were deliberately excluded.

At lower levels, and subject to the observance of agreed procedure, the author would leave the choice of a candidate to the standing committee concerned with the service or department. If the department serves several committees it is well for the staff committee to make the appointment— or to secure the Council's consent to an arrangement for appointments to be left to a joint sub-committee of the staff committee and other committees concerned.

In regard to cases of discipline, he would leave any initial investigation necessary at committee level to the committee concerned with the department or service in which the officer is engaged, or to a joint sub-committee if there is more than one; and leave the staff committee, or, in the case of large Authorities, a sub-committee of it, to be the domestic tribunal of appeal contemplated by Article 15 of the Charter.

A third category of business in which there may be some room both for differences of opinion and practice is that of changes in, or additions to, the establishment. It may be assumed that the initial formulation of the establishment will be dealt with by the staff committee and is of the very essence of its work. It is also a fairly safe assumption that few staff committees would address themselves to this work without inviting either the initial recommendations of the standing committees dealing with the services, or the observations of such committees on proposals initially formulated by the staff committee. The real issue arises in connection with proposed changes in grading, or additions to the list. The author would take the bold course, and place these in the hands of the staff committee for consideration on reports tendered to it direct by the departmental heads concerned, with any observations of the Clerk of the Authority thereon, or of any establishment officer who may be appointed to his staff. In the case of proposed additions to the establishment, and even in some proposals for regrading, the prosposals will usually arise out of questions as to ways and means of discharging new tasks or of dealing with varying levels of work, topics on which it will in any event have been the duty of the chief officer concerned to report to the committee dealing with the service. In these circumstances, it would seem that the situation could ordinarily be met if the chief officer, when reporting to the committee on the general questions, gave then an indication that staffing questions were involved, and indicated in general terms the nature of the recommendations he would be submitting to the establishment committee.

Subject to the foregoing considerations, the author would entrust all other questions relating to the conditions, recruitment, qualification, training and promotion of the staff to the staff committee. The question of what powers, if any, the staff committee should have to handle them is part of the general question involved in Local Authority administration as to the powers to be delegated to committees, or reserved to the Council, and should be pursued in studies on Local Authority administration. It may be necessary to add that, as in practically every type of authority a system of budgetary control is operative which involves the submission of proposals of committees dealing with particular services to the finance committee in certain eventualities, there will be some need to define the relationship of the staffs committee to the finance committee. It is impossible to think it necessary for any kind of staff business to be routed through three committees. If the Council approves of an addition to the establishment on the recommendations of a central committee such as its staff committee, it is unreasonable for the finance committee to ask for such a specific proposal to be submitted to it as well, under financial standing orders. The whole object of the procedure under financial standing orders is to bring up such an item for special scrutiny. This is, in fact, secured through the functions of the establishment committee, when it deals centrally with the staff requirements of all committees and departments. There is no reason why the staff committee should not, however, be asked for its views as to the global estimate to be made for the year, and required to lay information before the finance committee as to the financial effect of new national awards or recommendations which it passes.

The Rôle of the Local Joint Committee

Further aspects of Local Authority staff management arise in the provision of facilities for representations to be made to the Authority by the staff, either collectively or individually. So far as the collective aspect is concerned, the situation is being met to an increasing extent by the establishment of local joint committees representative of the Authority and the staff organizations concerned, which are in fact extensions of the Whitley machine to the local level. As matters stand, these local joint committees are not a compulsory element of the general Whitley machinery, in the sense that they are recognized by the constitutions of either the National Joint Council or the Provincial Council, or that they are an agency covenanted for in the agreement between the employers and employees which led to the establishment of the National and Provincial Councils. In the negotiations for the Charter, however, the parties did agree to commend suitable provision for joint consultation at local level between the Local Authorities and their staff through the medium of local joint committees. The recommendation has in fact since been repeated in the recent *Survey* of the National Joint Council, to which earlier reference has been made, and shows that local joint committees have in fact been established in a majority of Local Authorities.

The National Joint Council has prepared and promulgated a model constitution for such bodies, both sides of the

Council having recognized the need for some suitable circumscription of the scope and functions of these local bodies having regard to the agreed jurisdiction of both the National Joint Council and the Provincial Councils. In general, it may be said that this model safeguards the functions of the National and Provincial Councils in respect of grading and classification. It safeguards also the prerogatives of the Local Authority in controlling its establishment, and precludes questions of individual discipline, promotion or efficiency from discussion in the local joint committee. But apart from these reserved matters, it affords a wide avenue for the discussion of staff grievances, the submission of staff representation of matters not covered by the National Scheme, and affords a useful avenue for dealing with any malaise which may enter into the relationships between a Council and its staff. The model includes provisions in regard to the constitution of decisions by a majority on both sides, similar to those in the constitutions of the Provincial and National Council, and there is provision for meetings to be called on requisition of either side. The representatives of the Council are usually drawn from the establishment committee where one is appointed. The chairman of the Council's establishment committee is often appointed chairman of the local joint committee; though in some instances provision is made for the employers and the staff to hold the chair in successive years, the leader of one side being appointed vice-chairman in the year when the leader of the other holds the chair.

The Work of the Establishment Officer

In a large Local Authority the work of staff management in all its aspects entails considerable work and study at the official level, and it is not surprising that many of the larger Authorities have appointed establishment officers, under whom much if not all of the work at official level can be consolidated, who can make the necessary study and analysis of questions which arise for determination by the Council and its committees, and who can give specialized advice in regard to some classes of employees. Specialist appointments of this character are thoroughly justified

L

when, as is usually the case, the duties extend not only to the Council's official staff but to its workmen.

Similar considerations arise, however, in regard to the role of such establishment officers in Local Government as arise in the sphere of private industry and business. A good deal of the work of the establishment officer raises no kind of administrative problem, as there are obvious advantages in large authorities in consolidating the secretarial, administrative and clerical work in the maintenance of records, the conduct of correspondence, etc.—a course, moreover, which often relieves hard-pressed higher officers from immersion in unnecessary detail. Many of the questions arising in connection with grading and establishment, however, are related to administrative considerations within the province of the executive officers or departmental heads concerned. Difficulties of an obvious kind could arise if the establishment officer has a status on a par with that of one of the chief administrative or executive officers; or if, though his status were lower, his position was independent and he was in a position to challenge their proposals on his own responsibility, while having no responsibility in the related questions of administration and execution of the Council's policy. Undoubtedly, the proposals of departmental heads should not escape scrutiny, and, generally speaking, the situation is met by making the establishment officer responsible to the Authority's Clerk, and indeed a member of his staff. In smaller Authorities some member of the Town Clerk's staff may be designated to discharge the essential functions of an establishment officer.

Responsibility to the Clerk was recommended by the Hadow Departmental Committee, which, even at that time, saw an emerging need for the appointment of establishment officers in larger Authorities (see paragraph 148). This arrangement is, of course, in keeping with the view recognized by practically all Local Authorities in practice, and in any event endorsed by the last Royal Commission on Local Government, by the Hadow Departmental Report of 1934, and again quite recently by Negotiating Committee A, that the Town Clerk is the Council's chief administrative and executive officer, with the duty of co-ordinating the Council's administrative machine. It is a sound view that whoever is concerned with general administrative oversight cannot divorce himself from the oversight of all fundamental issues arising in regard to staff, and particularly those which are organically related to administrative aim or method. One thing inevitably involves the other. In the system of Local Government the other chief officers have, of course, their own administrative and executive responsibilities for the work of their departments. It is not suggested that the Clerk to a local Authority should seek to interfere in a departmental head's assessment of his staffing needs in the light of clearly recognizable executive and technical tasks. The Clerk must surely, however, be conceded the right to tender his observations on staffing questions which raise questions of administrative principle and co-ordination, or raise obvious issues of balance and uniformity between departmental requirements of a common character. To facilitate the discharge of his higher functions on staffing questions it is proper that in large Authorities he should have the help of an establishment officer, furnishing administrative and secretarial help and assisting in the analysis of issues. There are, no doubt, many matters of executive detail which can be settled at official level, and in fact dealt with largely by the establishment officer, but it is desirable that he should have the quickest access to the senior officer involved, namely, the Clerk of the Authority, and be in a position to exercise his functions with the proper backing at the highest level of official responsibility.

This chapter affords but a very broad outline of the very extensive and complex work which falls to the Local Authority and its appropriate officers in the sphere of staff management. There is much room for more detailed study in this field, and we commend therefore the enterprise of the Institute of Public Administration in organizing on two successive occasions conferences on Local Authority personnel management and draw attention to the reports of these conferences published by the Institute, and to the booklet subsequently prepared by a study group of the Institute, *Local Government Establishment Work*—which are listed in the Bibliography.

PART THREE

QUALIFICATIONS AND TRAINING

CHAPTER IX

Basic Requirements

It is proposed, in this concluding part of our work, to review the arrangements now operating in the Service for qualification and training, and to discuss such major questions as arise in regard to them. In this present chapter we deal with those levels of the Service, for the most part subordinate, which fall within the scope of the National Joint Council and its associated agency, the Local Government Examinations Board. In the following chapter we deal with the qualifications and training of chief officers.

The situation is not the same at the two levels. In the one case the requirements of the Local Authorities are being guided on the national plane by the National Joint Council and the Board, whose work rests upon an accepted view as to the needs of the Service and an agreed policy for meeting those needs. At the level of the chief officers much still rests upon the practice of the Local Authorities, acting upon their own responsibility at a local level. Any criticism there may be of the kind of qualifications and training which Local Authorities look for in their chief officers lacks any organized expression of the kind which has entered into the work and decisions of the National Joint Council and the Local Government Examinations Board in relation to the subordinate grades.

As was said earlier on, the Charter is not, in itself, an exhaustive code for qualifications and training, and although those provisions in it which deal with this subject are obviously aimed at certain existing deficiencies and certain prospective needs, they contain no statement of the philosophy which informs them. The Local Government Examinations Board, since its establishment, has secured the National Council's approval to many arrangements which expand those provisions, but even in the documents which embody the Board's supplementary schemes, as approved by the National Joint Council, there is much that is implied rather than expressed as to the needs they are designed to meet and the line of policy adopted. This is understandable, because the outward expression of the Board's work has often to take the form of rules and regulations; whereas the formative documents are of a domestic character, passing in circles which understand the nature of the work, and recognize or take for granted the assumptions made. In consequence, the Board's aims are not always easily visible; and the outside observer who seeks enlightenment by studying the Boards' formal schemes is in some danger of not seeing the wood for the trees. With these considerations in mind it has been thought best to approach the whole subject by clearing the ground through a preliminary analysis of the requirements of the Service, and of the conditions on which these requirements have to be met.

A Preliminary Analysis

It is generally agreed that recruitment to the officer classes at the junior level calls for a certain standard of general education, and that, in considering what the minimum standard shall be, two considerations have to be borne in mind. Even if the destiny of the junior entrant may reach no further than the General Division, in which the duties do not extend beyond the less responsible kind of clerical work, these duties are nevertheless of a kind which require a sound schooling. In addition, the standard should also have regard to the needs beyond the General Division, and be such as to afford a mental training which will enable the officer to proceed to the further studies involved in 'qualifications' without any major scholastic teaching.

For the professional and technical grades the requirement can briefly and broadly be stated as being, that for professional and technical work the appropriate professional or technical qualifications should be required. What is an appropriate qualification is a question not open to much doubt when it comes to the engagement of lawyers, doctors, and even accountants. The question is, however, a much more difficult one in relation to narrower but quite specialized fields of professional or technical work, and, as we shall see, the valuation of qualification in these fields has entered into the question of eligibility for promotion, and has had to be dealt with by the National Joint Council and the Examinations Board.

The remaining classes to be considered are those above the General Division but who are not professional or technical officers.

It is the requirements to be made of this residue which have in fact engaged most of the time and attention of the Local Government Examinations Board since its establishment under the Charter; for underneath the Charter provision for a Promotion Examination lay the recognition that the existence of this largely unqualified residue was the main defect of the Local Government Service. Many outside observers, including the Hadow Committee itself, had stressed this defect. N.A.L.G.O. had sought to remedy it by its own examination; but wanted some examination of higher prestige if only to open up advancement to officers who had entered the Service on the bottom rung of the ladder but were faced with the obstacles that lay in the path of professional qualification.

But, as the Board has realized, the requirements to be made of this residue are not one and the same, but several and different. The residue is a very mixed one. The Charter had provided for the grouping of staff into Divisions, specified in the terms we quoted earlier on. But these terms were wide, and in the subsequent process of classification by each Local Authority on implementing the Charter there was considerable latitude for the continuance of past practice on the part of the individual Authority, and for the retention of past status by serving officers to which the Charter had initially to be applied. In this way, the distinction between the Clerical and the Higher Clerical Divisions, on the one hand, and the lower ranges of the A.P.T. Grades, on the other, became blurred. Moreover, the fact that the same scales had been adopted in the Charter for the administrative professional and technical Staffs alike led to the conception of one A.P.T. Division. The Charter in fact styles the Division as a single one for all three classes. Distinctions have been further blurred by the variable gradings accorded to some semi-technical posts, and to posts of a kind which in the Civil Service would be classed in the executive officer grades. Posts of this latter kind are of higher status than those suited to the Clerical or Higher Clerical Divisions but the Charter made no specific provision for them.

But even if we disregard cases of doubtful classification, the Administrative Section of the A.P.T. Division remains not only mixed in composition but comprised of very disparate levels. Taken as a whole, it obviously does not constitute an administrative class of the same kind as that which is so styled in the Civil Service. It has not been so conceived of. Its 'ceiling' stops short of all the higher posts in the Service; and its first grade commencing at a salary of £315 a year (at the original Charter rate) could hardly apply to any post whatsoever of real administrative function, despite the definition of administrative function which is attached to the Division, and which follows that for the administrative class of the Civil Service.

On the other hand, while chief officers in the large and medium-sized Authorities, and in some instances their deputies and principal assistants, come above the National Joint Council's 'ceiling', in the smaller Authorities they come beneath it and are accommodated in the higher grades of the A.P.T. Division. The middle and lower ranges of the A.P.T. scales accommodate, on the other hand, many principal assistants whose function is administrative, e.g. deputies in the medium-sized or smaller authorities, and who may possess the same professional qualification as their chiefs, along with others such as committee clerks whose function is administrative, but for whom no qualification was available before those set up by the Examinations Board. The middle ranges of the A.P.T. Division in particular accommodate many officers whose duties are indubitably administrative, and are, like those of the committee clerk, of a very responsible character; and even prior to the Charter requirements many of these officers had taken, by post entry study, one or other of the Diplomas in Public Administration. This confused position is to some extent being relieved by the supplementary Charter for miscellaneous officers, which will abstract from the A.P.T. Divisions some officers whose duties are not really administrative (still less professional or technical) and it may be that the administrative class will be still further segregated if the Council introduces a classification similar to that of the executive officer in the Civil Service.

Looked at broadly, the situation is one which obviously calls for differentiation in post-entry qualifications and promotion tests. As matters stand, the Clerical and Higher Clerical Divisions (and any new executive class) have requirements different from and of less standard than the administrative Division. If the administrative Division is to be segregated and perform a function truly administrative, if its personnel are to be able to look their professional brethren in the face, there should be attached to it a qualification or promotion test of high standard. It is a further inference, that if the Local Government Service is to retain its existing structure, and if there is to be a ladder of opportunity for the serving officer, this qualification or test must be in stages, designed to accommodate officers at the lower and the higher levels, with some connection between the stages which fits them into one course of continuous and progressive study. Such a line of thought is the one at which the Local Government Examinations Board has in fact now arrived, and which animates the scheme we notice later.

Having broadly stated the requirements of various groups and levels of the Service, it remains to add that there are certain requirements which are common to them all, chief officers included. The concept of an efficient service, variously composed, but functioning as one organism, calls for knowledge, at all levels, of the structure, organization, and function of the Local Government System itself. To an increasing extent, all public services, and all major industries and large-scale business units, are recognizing the need for a similar diffusion of a corresponding knowledge throughout all groups and levels of the personnel they employ, and not merely at the top—a need which could be illustrated by many analyses of what is involved in efficient management, adequate response to public or consumer need, and teamwork by the staff to ensure these objects. The degree of knowledge required is obviously different at differing levels. An elementary knowledge is called for even at the level of a clerk. At the level of the chief officer, the measure of knowledge should be intimate, extensive, and profound, and should extend to a knowledge of the environment, in the way of economic, social, and political conditions, in which the system has to work and administration be carried out. Between these two extreme levels the need is still there, in varying measure, and extends to the professional and technical officer who finds himself in an administrative environment and has to co-operate with administrative colleagues. We shall not begin to understand some of the work of the Local Government Examinations Board in regard to qualifications or the views it takes in regard to syllabuses for various examinations, unless we realize that this need, too, is one which it has had in mind.

To set even the broad pattern of qualification for a service so varied is obviously no easy task in itself, but it is rendered the more difficult by some of the circumstances which must condition it. The task involves, in the first place, a great deal of adjustment to the interests and functions of numerous agencies extraneous to the world of Local Government— education authorities, universities, professional institutes, and Government Departments. Schemes for standards of entry must be adjusted to the educational system of the country. In seeking appropriate qualifications for the specific tasks of the Service, there must often be some suitable adjustment of curricula to those of the main professional bodies. To some extent these are prepared to orientate their curricula to the needs of a particular service or occupational environment, but there must surely be limits beyond which they cannot go, for the aim of established professions is to provide a minimum equipment of knowledge and training adaptable to all spheres of employment. As to the relation of service qualifications to university teaching, the situation is complicated by current differences of opinion as to what the function of university teaching is in modern society, but, however much some authorities now lean to studies broadly related to particular fields of human effort, few of them would go to the length of countenancing teaching for particular 'outside' qualifications. And, finally, behind all questions as to what should be the particular studies for particular sections of the Service lies the need to be sure that teaching facilities are available—a consideration which is found in many instances to impose appreciable limits upon the type of syllabus that can be introduced.

Junior Entry

The Charter sought to establish throughout the Service entry by examination at the qualifying level of the General School Certificate. Broadly, the prescription followed practice introduced between the two wars, and in some areas even earlier, by the more progressive Local Authorities, many of which, indeed, required Matriculation as the qualifying standard. The examination was to be in two stages, the first a qualifying stage, and the second competitive, the latter to include competitive interview. That the qualifying standard should be tested by further examination was a requirement designed no doubt to give a chance to the candidate from the elementary school who might have continued studies after leaving school, the School Certificate Examination being essentially a secondary-school test. There was obviously something to be said for exempting from this preliminary stage the candidate who had actually taken the School Certificate, if, as appears to have been the intention, the competitive stage was to comprise an examination in the academic sense of the term; but this course was, on balance, not favoured.

As a universal prescription, the Charter provision broke down. This is not to say that Local Authorities which had held competitive examinations, or required the School Certificate standard, abandoned their requirements; but all of them reported a lack of candidates of anything like the calibre which they had obtained before the war. The staff organizations alleged that the Charter rates were inadequate, and it is clear in retrospect that they were in many parts of the country unattractive. But it must also be acknowledged that the Service was suffering from post-war conditions which affected in the same way public services and industries which had looked for the same standards, and often paid more.

The chief factor which militated against any attempt to enforce the Charter clause and preserve the standard contemplated was, however, the change in educational policy which occurred almost as soon as the ink was dry on the Charter provision, involving the abolition of the School Certificate as a scholastic test. The standard could no longer be expressed in terms of the School Certificate. During the years immediately after 1946 the Board was unable to formulate any alternative until it was known exactly when the School Certificate would go and what was to take its place. The School Certificate came to an end in 1951, and in 1950 the Board was able to review the position, and approved an alternative arrangement, but was careful to describe this as only an interim one.

The School Certificate required a satisfactory standard in a minimum number of school subjects. The new General Certificate of education is one which certifies the standard reached in such subjects as the pupil had elected to take, which may be only one or two. It is not for us to discuss the philosophy of the change. Briefly, the argument was that school education was being bent too much to the pattern of examination requirements, particularly those of a grammar school or matriculation type. As to the requirements of particular employers, the argument seems to be that they would have to impose their own requirements, as indeed the universities very quickly decided to do. It seems clear that such a course is the only one before the Local Government Service if it seeks to preserve in new terms the kind of standard contemplated by the Charter. The Board's recommendation, since approved by the National Joint Council, takes this line, and provides for a qualifying examination in four subjects, English, Mathematics, and two others, as certified by the General Certificate, or as tested in an examination to be conducted by the Board. The Board, having now recognized that the Provincial Councils are not equipped to undertake examination arrangements, propose to hold the examination themselves at the request of Local Authorities.

Broadly, the intention behind the detailed arrangements seems to be to maintain what may broadly be described as the secondary-school standard, though for an interim period it looks as though this standard will in fact be somewhat lower than that maintained by many Local Authorities before the war. Certainly nothing less than the secondary-school standard would suffice, and it is to be hoped that something like the standard originally contemplated by the Charter can be restored. There are no doubt classes of simple clerical work in the Service which can be performed by entrants at a lower standard of general education; but by and large the elementary-school standard was found inadequate in the past. Entrants should be equipped to move from one grade of work to another, as the Charter intends that they should do, and this on grounds both of efficiency and training. Experience has shown that nothing less than the secondary-school standard, and an age level of sixteen years for entry, produces the type of entrant which makes this kind of mobility possible, or who is free from major handicap in proceeding to serious post-entry studies.

The Original Promotion Examination

The clause in the Charter prescribing a promotion examination said nothing about its character or standard, or anything except in negative terms about its function. It was to be a bar on promotion from the General Grade,—i.e. no one was to be considered eligible for promotion unless he passed the examination or possessed a recognized professional or technical qualification. The terms of the Charter clearly envisaged the promotion examination as one examination, conferring eligibility for promotion to all the grades above the General Division on staff not possessing or proceeding to professional or technical qualifications. This, of course, is not to say that the passing of the examination of itself effected a transfer to a higher grade, and the terms of the Charter clause made it clear that promotion would depend on a vacancy arising in the higher grades and on personal qualities.

The considerations mentioned in the introductory analysis to this chapter as to the mixed nature, and the mixed requirements of the A.P.T. Grades were not, it would appear, very clearly grasped by those who framed the Charter clause relating to the promotion examination: but the Board addressed itself to its task, and in 1947 devised an examination syllabus. The first examination was held in 1948, the National Council agreeing to certain dispensations for older officers already in the Service. Further examinations were held in 1949 and 1950.

Following the line advocated in the Hadow Report (see paragraphs 125 and 129) the examination took the broad character of an administrative examination. The syllabus required five papers, taken at one sitting: a compulsory paper in English, and two compulsory papers covering the broad field of Local and Central Government; a fourth paper on a subject chosen from seven alternative general background subjects; and a fifth paper chosen from the field of background subjects, or from the field of departmental study, such as finance, education, or social welfare.

In the first two years the standard of the competitors was disappointing, but there was a noticeable improvement in 1950. At no time, however, had the number of successful competitors sufficed to meet the recruitment needs of the Authorities for the classes above the General Division; and the National Joint Council had been forced to sanction successive relaxations of the Charter requirement that no General Grade officer could be promoted without having passed the examination or its equivalent.

In 1950 the Board reviewed its experience of the Examination and reported that it had come to the conclusion that a new approach would have to be made. In the advice it tendered to the National Joint Council there was a clear implication that the deficiency in numbers passing the

Promotion Examination was not quite the reflection on the non-professional and sectional elements of the Service that at first sight it appeared to be. In point of fact, most observers who had reviewed the syllabus and the first results of the Promotion Examination were agreed that the standard exacted was surprisingly high for the majority of the officers who were expected to take the test. The character of the examination was not any different from that of the university diplomas in public administration, and many competent observers thought, and said, that the standard of the papers was higher than that for most of the diploma examinations. In its own review of the position, the Board tacitly acknowledged that the examination was in fact too exacting as a test for admission to the Clerical and Higher Clerical Grades. On the other hand, the Board felt that the examination could not be regarded as an adequate test to establish eligibility for the whole range of the administrative section of the A.P.T. Grades. If the existing examination was too stiff as a test for admission to the clerical grades, it was too easy as a test of eligibility for senior administrative posts.

The New Clerical and Administrative Examinations

Following upon the review of 1950, the Board secured the approval of the National Joint Council to a complete recasting of the promotion test. For the Clerical and Higher Clerical Divisions, a new clerical examination was introduced. For the Administrative Grades—which the Board stressed should in future be regarded as a segregated Division —a new administrative examination was established in two stages—an intermediate stage conferring eligibility up to Grade IV, and a final stage conferring eligibility beyond. The final stage of the administrative examination was to be regarded as conferring an administrative qualification equivalent in status and standard to that of the major professional qualifications, and to be of no lower standard than a university pass-degree.

There can be no doubt that the Board's new policy was sound. A division of the tests for the Clerical and Administrative Divisions, respectively, was obviously necessary. To

M

provide an administrative examination in two stages was a practical way of catering for the gradations of the Administrative Division as it exists; while the fact that the two stages are related parts of one total syllabus affords a sound course of progressive study for administrative officers. Whether the standard of the final examination will, in fact, be such as to deserve and win the same prestige for the examination as the professional qualifications remains to be seen. Whether the examination will in practice confer eligibility for chief officership may be a matter for doubt, though such an idea is undoubtedly in the minds of those responsible for the changed policy. But even if it stops short of these attainments, the new administrative examination should do much to secure the more satisfactory training of the non-professional officer who assumes fairly responsible administrative duties. It should also, in time, enlarge the opportunities of the officer with the administrative qualification, if, as may well happen, the existence of a new layer of qualified non-professional officers induces Local Authorities to make a clearer segregation of work as between the professional and the administrative officers.

Following upon the elaboration of detailed syllabuses and regulations for the new examinations, the Board appointed April 1951 as the date for the first clerical examination, October 1951 for the first Intermediate Administrative Examination, and April 1952 for the Final Administrative Examination.

The syllabus for the Clerical examination requires three papers of three hours each, one in English (or Welsh) and two in the outlines of Local and Central Government respectively.

The syllabus for the intermediate stage of the administrative examination requires three compulsory papers of three hours each, one in English, and two covering the broad field of Local and Central Government; a fourth paper chosen from 'mental discipline' or 'tool' subjects, i.e. Economics, Mathematics, Statistics, Logic and Scientific Method; and a fifth paper chosen from a group of five background subjects, namely, Social and Economic History since 1760, the Constitutional History of England,

Constitutional Law of England, the Elements of English Law, and Regional and Physical Geography.

The final stage of the administrative examination is in two parts, which may be taken separately. In Part I, three compulsory papers are required, i.e. in Principles and Problems of Public Administration (General), Principles and Problems of Public Administration (Local Government), and the Social Services. In Part II two papers are required, one chosen from a group of subjects styled Group A and comprising Social and Political Theory, Political Institutions, Social Statistics, Economics of Public Finance, Administrative Law, and Nationalized Industries Administration; and one further paper chosen from Group B comprising Local Government Law, Local Government Finance, Education, Public Health, or the Administration of a particular Department or sphere of Local Authority activity.

The Recognition of Professional Qualifications

Just as prescriptions with a wide impact upon the non-professional ranks in the Service have resulted from the work of the National Joint Council and the Examinations Board in implementing the Charter clause relating to the Promotion Examination, so also has the clause given rise to important developments in another direction, namely, the recognition to be afforded to a variety of professional examinations. And just as the clause led the Examinations Board into a false start in dealing with tests for the non-professional staffs, so also did it lead the Board into a false start in this complementary task. It required the General Division Officer if he did not pass the Promotion Examination to have 'secured such qualification as is recognized by the Local Government Examinations Board as an alternative to the Promotion Examination'. When the Charter was negotiated a wide range of professional qualifications was already recognized. Some had an established national status. Others were of the narrower specialist kind mostly confined to the Local Government field itself; and while among the latter class some were of rather dubious status the majority were, of their kind, quite good, and involved

serious studies. What was mostly lacking was, as we have
seen, a suitable test for the administrative and clerical
staffs, and the main object of the clause was to establish
one. This being so, the wording of the clause may be thought
curious. It seemed to regard the Promotion Examination
(notwithstanding that it had yet to be established) as the
normal test, and professional qualifications in general as
only substitutes. On the other hand, the phrasing of the
clause may be explained by a feeling on the part of the
Charter negotiators that 'professional' qualifications in the
Local Government Service were of very unequal standard
and stood in need of some review, and that if both the
Promotion Examination and qualifications of a professional
kind were to confer eligibility for appointment above
General Division it was necessary to ensure that there should
be no 'easy options'.

To assess 'alternatives' to a Promotion Examination is, of
course, rather different from attempting to assess the value
of particular qualifications in terms of the work required.
As matters stand, this latter function is still the prerogative
of the Local Authority. In any event, no assessment of this
latter kind was possible when the Board approached its task
of determining the alternatives. Both in assessing equivalents
(meaning by that term examinations or qualifications
appropriate to the administrative and clerical staff for which
the Promotion Examination was instituted), and in assessing
alternatives (meaning by that term professional and technical examinations) the Board could rightly have looked at
standards of study and the time and effort involved in
qualification. It had in fact little more to go upon.

In producing, however, in 1947, its 'First List of Examinations Recognized for Promotion Purposes', the Board
revealed, in the preface to this document, quite an unexpected desideratum which had entered into its decisions.
The passing of professional qualifications should not, the
Board thought, be allowed to eliminate the need for the
officer to study at the outset the subjects relating to Local
Government structure and functions contained in the
syllabus for the Promotion Examination. The Board's aim,

therefore, was in effect to orientate the syllabus for all professional examinations, so as to provide the officer in the first stages of his professional studies with a knowledge of Local Government and its constitutional and administrative mechanisms. In pursuit of this objective the Board laid it down that no intermediate professional qualification would count as an equivalent or alternative to the Promotion Examination. Now we ourselves in the introduction to this chapter have stated that knowledge of this kind is desirable in some measure at all levels of the Service; but the attempt of the Board to secure it in this way was open to much criticism.

The Board had to admit, in its preface to the List, that the full examination of many of the professional qualifications constituted a much more arduous course of study than that for the Promotion Examination. The general grade officer developing a definite occupational bent was thus tempted to defer his professional qualification by taking an easier and quicker course in advance as a means to speedy but more limited promotion. And this notwithstanding the fact that, above the level of the General Division and the clerical classes, the Service requires more officers with an executive function than officers with an administrative function, and that in the post-war years there was a grave and continuing shortage of qualified staff in the professional, technical and specialist sections of the Service.

But these were not the most weighty objections to the Board's approach. Apart from its effect, a policy of inducing all the professional institutes to modify their intermediate syllabus to include the 'Service' subjects of the Promotion Examination was as intrinsically unsound as it was unrealistic. For the many posts in the Service which call for the best kind of professional qualification, the prime consideration, in providing a supply of qualified recruits, should be the essential professional studies. At the stage of the *final* examination many of the major professional bodies do orientate their syllabuses in some measure to particular occupational fields. The extent to which that can be done must always be a matter of nice judgment. The professional qualifications that are the most valuable, which provide the most comprehensive training, and command the highest respect, are those which provide a qualification based upon wide but essentially professional study, affording a minimum but wide equipment for all occupational fields, and not merely one. The attempt to orientate all professional syllabuses at intermediate level was entirely wrong, because it is precisely at that level that the student for a major profession should concentrate upon the basic professional studies. There may be some instances, e.g. the narrower or purely Local Government specialisms, in which such a course might reasonably have been followed; and in these instances the Board would have been on firm ground in seeking something of a common content for the intermediate stages of these examinations and the compulsory subjects of the Promotion Examination. But as the List will show, the Board's policy was quite undiscriminating in this respect. Had it persisted in its attempt it must soon have realized that to ask the established professional bodies to accept its policy was to chase the moon. The Board had complained in its preface that some of the professional qualifications relating to the Service as such were too narrow and specialized. There is truth in that statement. But does not one get to a similar and perhaps more dangerous kind of narrow specialism if broad professional examinations are perverted to suit the requirements of a particular (and in many respects a peculiar) occupational field? Not only the Local Government Service itself, but the nation at large, stands to lose a great deal if professional qualifications are orientated too much in this way. Occupational specialisms can be pursued after qualification.

In the substituted list of equivalent examinations which the Board produced after the establishment of the new clerical and administrative examinations, the initial policy was abandoned. The Board in effect acknowledged its error.

To the new clerical examination the Board admits no equivalent or alternative whatever. This policy can be justified in that here there is no question of a competing professional or other higher qualification, and on the other hand, a knowledge of the essential mechanisms of Local Government as required by the two papers on Central and Local Government, and a command of English tested by the English paper, can be regarded as the minimum and essential equipment of the higher grade clerk.

In its treatment of the professional examinations the List is entirely different from the first one. Not all intermediates are recognized, but many are. Some claimants have been rejected. The Board has attempted an assessment of the value and status of many of the professional examinations of the narrower kind, and expressed this in terms which limit the eligibility for promotion to certain levels only in the administrative division, while conferring eligibility up to its full range in other cases. There may be some dubious aspects even about this new approach, but pending some more objective and thorough assessment of qualifications in terms of the duties required, it is a reasonable and practical one in the face of existing conditions. It is only fair to say also that the Board's evaluations have been accepted by the National Joint Council, comprised as it is of two sides, bringing to bear a variety of experience and knowledge. The beginning must of necessity be somewhat rough and ready in a field so diverse, and the Board will no doubt keep the List well under review and be prepared to vary it in the light of experience and of any improvements in the status and standards of the examinations which confer only a limited eligibility for promotion.

University Teaching in Public Administration

The normal range of university teaching in modern times has extended to many studies deemed valuable for those concerned with government and administration. Such courses as 'Modern Greats' at Oxford and some of the studies for degrees in Philosophy, Economics, and Law are cases in point. In the course of the last twenty years, however, most of our universities have established courses and instituted qualifications which are related to administrative training rather more directly. London set the example in 1928 by instituting both an Internal and an External Diploma in

Public Administration, the latter open to matriculated students and others who were accepted on having attained a satisfactory standard of education. Later, the University decided to require matriculation for the External as well as the Internal Diploma, but introduced a Diploma in the Extra-mural Department for non-matriculated students whose educational standard could be accepted on consideration of the individual case. Liverpool quickly followed suit with its own Internal Diploma, and in the period between the two wars similar qualifications were instituted by most of the other provincial universities, often on the solicitation of N.A.L.G.O., and with grants from that body in aid of staffing costs. Manchester introduced Degrees, B.A. and M.A. (Admin.); Oxford introduced at first only a Certificate but later a Diploma.

Though there is considerable variation in the content of the syllabuses, that originally adopted by London affords some idea of the field of study for qualifications of this kind. Part I comprised three compulsory papers of three hours each—Public Administration (Central and Local), Economics, including Public Finance, and Social and Political Theory. Part II comprised three papers of three hours each, at least one to be chosen from two groups, Group A being English Constitutional Law, English Economic and Social History Since 1760, and the Constitutional History of Great Britain Since 1783, and Group B being Statistics, the History and Principles of Local Government, and Social Administration. In the early years London required the passing of an oral examination for external students, following upon the written examination, but later withdrew this requirement.

Both in instituting qualifications of this kind and in providing teaching for them, the course followed by the universities has been of inestimable public benefit. For the most part the courses have been taken by serving officers (preponderantly drawn from the Local Government Service) and there may well have been some reciprocal benefit to the university teaching staffs in contacts with students of mature mind and practical experience in the field. The benefit to the efficiency of the Local Government Service has been enormous. The new qualifications stimulated post-entry study in every direction. They provided a valuable adjunct to the qualifications of the professional men in the Service, and one of particular value to the younger men moving up to higher appointments involving administrative function. Above all, they set attainable targets for the non-professional officer, afforded a mental training and serviceable background knowledge to the non-professional officers in the Administrative and Clerical Grades, and held out to these latter a qualification of some standing.

All this is not to say that the establishment of the Diplomas or Degrees has everywhere been productive of the same success. Despite the identity of titles, there seems little doubt that the qualification in one university is not in standard what it is in another. The original standard of the London Diploma was high, hardly less than a pass-degree. Liverpool claims that it has maintained this standard throughout, and that its Diploma is fully equivalent to the Degree of Manchester. A recent review conducted by university teachers interested in the field has indeed revealed not only considerable variations in syllabus content, but rather glaring disparities in standard, one illustration of which is that the course for the Diploma is one of two years in some universities and three years in others. Some universities have realized that in their commendable desire to offer opportunity to the clerical and non-professional and subordinate administrative assistants they have been led too far in the relaxation of the more formal educational tests for entry to the courses. London, a year or two ago, feeling overwhelmed by large numbers of entrants whose work proved them to be handicapped by a defective general education, revised its rules and tightened up its tests for entry, with the intention of restoring the Internal and External Diplomas to their original standards of post-graduate Diplomas for those with degrees or major professional qualifications. Other university Authorities are expected to take similar steps; and the university teachers themselves are making moves to improve where necessary the standards of the Diploma courses and establish greater uniformity.

The new administrative examination of the Local Government Examination Board, and the Board's policy in directing it, will have an obvious impact on the Diplomas and Degrees of the universities. Until the new examinations have been held, and it is seen how the conception of its standard and syllabus works out in practice, it is too soon to say what that impact will be, or to what extent the university examinations will be recognized as a total or partial equivalent. At the moment, the Board's examination will, as planned, be the more onerous. It is somewhat wider in range, aimed at Degree or professional standard, and the papers in Public Administration are intended, it is understood, to go beyond background knowledge, bear directly on specific administrative problems, and involve more 'realistic' study than is said to be usual in the university courses. The Board has, of course, already been called upon to make some immediate arrangements as to the account to be taken of Diplomas which officers already possess or for which they are now studying. It has decided to defer a settlement of the final relationship between the two qualifications for a period of five years, one which should afford the universities the opportunity of improving standards where necessary and perhaps making some adjustments in syllabus which may make the Diplomas a recognized alternative if not to the whole of the Board's examination then to some substantial portion of it. To those officers who take a Diploma before 1955 and who have also five years' experience in an administrative post, the Board has given an exemption from its own examination. Short of the latter requirement the Diploma will confer eligibility up to grade IV.

Influenced perhaps by Civil Service practice, the Board has, for good or ill, taken the line that the Service should have its own administrative examination, moulded to its specific requirements. There are some who may regret this course, and feel that as the universities had gone so far in meeting service requirements they might well have been urged to go further; and since it is they in the main who will still be drawn upon for teaching in the subjects of the Board's examination, and since the problem of teaching, for any of the 'realistic' studies in the Board's syllabus is one not yet fully solved, much could be said for conserving university interest and aiding university effort in establishing a university qualification which could fulfil the same function as the administrative examination. On the other hand, present conditions have called for speedy action, and to give a service job to a service agency may be the speediest way.

Various Forms of Training

We have thought it best to concentrate in present conditions on the kind of training involved in qualification, but the importance of other forms of training should be recognized, even if they cannot be fully discussed here. One of the most important is the internal and departmental training that can be offered immediately after entry. In the Local Government Service, as elsewhere, what has been done has sadly lagged behind the needs of the situation; the truth being that the last twelve years of continuous crisis have imposed a pressure on senior officers which has precluded them from devoting personal time to the task. For the professional grades the professional institutes provide a variety of facilities for the discussion of subjects and problems at an advanced and specialist level. Some have special discussion circles for students. N.A.L.G.O. caters for all groups in the Service by dealing with subjects of general interest to the Service in courses and lectures at its summer and week-end schools. Some Local Authorities are including Local Government studies in the curricula of adult residential colleges under the statutory provisions for further education; and the courses of the Workers' Educational Association and the extra-mural departments of the universities, though 'non-vocational', absorb many students drawn from the Service. Finally, the Institute of Public Administration—a body originally formed on the initiative of Civil Servants and Local Government officers—is fulfilling an invaluable function for senior officers through the medium of its Journal, its lectures, its discussion groups, its research activities, and its publications. The whole field, if it were mapped out in detail, would present an untidy picture, no doubt, but on the whole a picture of busy and sustained effort which argues no little faith in the value and virtues of Local Government and a commendable sense of vocation on the part of the officers who participate in all these activities in such respectable numbers.

CHAPTER X

Requirements for High Office

IN ENUMERATING the principal officers, and describing the character of the offices which they hold (see Chapter II), we also noted the qualifications which they usually possess; and the reader will have observed that these qualifications were of the type generally described as professional. The Town Clerk, we found, was usually a solicitor, the Chief Financial Officer an accountant, the Engineer or Surveyor a professional engineer with recognized qualifications in the field of civil engineering and surveying, and the Medical Officer of Health a 'duly qualified medical practitioner'. Nor is the Chief Education Officer the exception which at first sight he seems to be; for although the primary qualification is ordinarily a university degree, Local Authorities usually require teaching experience in addition, and while they do not always go to the length of requiring the Chief Education Officer to have been a certificated teacher, the tendency has been in that direction. As we have seen, there are one or two instances in which qualifications are prescribed by statute or by statutory regulations. The requirement that a Medical Officer of Health shall be a duly qualified medical practitioner and shall also hold a Diploma in Public Health is of this kind. In general, however, the requirements rest upon Local Authority practice. Practice has attained, however, to such consistency and generality as to justify a broad proposition that a professional qualification is a requisite for the highest office in the Local Government Service.

Contrast with the Civil Service

In this respect, the Local Government Service stands in strong contrast with the Civil Service. The highest officers of the Civil Service are drawn from a segregated administrative class, and for the most part possess no professional qualification. Until fairly recently this class was recruited almost exclusively from the universities by competitive examination, normally at the age of twenty-three or twenty-four, the examination being academic in character and the effective qualifying standard being that of an Honours degree. In recent years, further tests have been introduced in the actual process of selection, such as preliminary interview, performance in group discussion, and formal interview by a board of interviewers. These pertain to the process of appointment and promotion rather than to the basic qualification with which we are concerned at the moment. Entry from the university in this way is still the main stream of recruitment. It has been possible for serving Civil Servants to take the prescribed examinations by post-entry study; in recent years there has been a reservation of places for serving officers; and officers who have worked their way up from the clerical to the 'executive' class, and shown ability, have been able to secure promotion to the administrative class without passing the normal examination.

The Civil Service has, of course, its corps of professional officers, variously classified in what are known as the professional grades. Despite the absence of any formal rule preventing the choice of a professional officer for high administrative office, there has in fact been a great gulf fixed between the professional grades and the administrative class; and rarely indeed has the professional officer been selected for high administrative office, or found it practicable to pass from his own class to the administrative class with that object in view. The Tomlin Commission expressed the opinion that in the nature of the case major administrative appointments were bound to be made for the most part from the administrative class, and appeared to take an acquiescent view of the situation. A later committee, however, recommended less rigidity of practice, and spoke of the loss to the Service in ignoring the additional field of choice for administrative positions which the professional grades provided.

The obvious contrast presented by the two services should not, however, lead us into the false inferences which are sometimes drawn. Beyond doubt, the administrative class of the Civil Service is, and was intended to be, the controlling class in the work of the Civil Service. And this fact, coupled with the strict segregation of the professional grades which has ruled hitherto, has led some people to the conclusion that the administrator is in his right place in the Civil Service in being 'at the top'; and that if in the Local Government Service the professional man is at the top then things are obviously wrong. The conclusion is demonstrably wrong and springs from a confusion of qualification with function. We may accept the postulate that in any large-scale organization with a variety of tasks, such as falls to both Central and Local Government and indeed large-scale industry, the administrative function must be paramount. Neither service, we may be sure, falls into the gross error of judging capacity for the highest administrative office by sole reference to either the professional qualification, in the one case, or to academic performance, in the other. If the needs of the two services are so similar as to call for some assessment of the respective merits of Civil Service and Local Government practice, then the real issues relate to the virtues of the two types of preparatory training, and the general adequacy of each main stream of recruitment to provide resources for the eventual choice of high administrative officers.

General Considerations in Basic Training

All this is not to say that argument is out of place in comparing the performance of the two services in achieving proper standards of administrative ability at the higher level. Nor does it remove argument about the wisdom of stereotyping, either in one service or another, and, whether by practice or prescription, the basic studies which can eventually lead to higher administrative office. If it be true that the capacity of the administrator must always in some measure depend upon his knowledge of the administrative milieu, some particular type of basic qualification or training may be found to contribute to this end. On the other hand, this factor may have to be discounted if it is found to have an unduly restrictive effect upon the field of choice. The balance may well depend upon the particular sector of administration which is in question.

There are some observers who will claim that neither service has yet hit upon the ideal basic training; and that, apart from post-entry training in its variety of forms, this should be sought in some specific 'administrative' qualification. It is difficult to see what other form this could take, at any rate for some time to come, than the passing of written examinations. While the value of qualifications in 'administration', in providing background knowledge and some grasp of theory, is incontestible, they have no better value as mental training than the older tests, whether professional or academic; and, at the age at which examinations are usually taken, professional studies are often more educative in the exercise of practical judgment. We should not have devoted so much of the last chapter to the 'administrative' examination of the universities and the Local Government Board if we had thought them unimportant or out of place in training for either Central or Local Government. But they should not be given a face value which is denied to the older tests merely because they are dubbed qualifications in administration. They raise many fundamental questions as to the extent to which 'administration' can really be taught, and how far it is possible, in purely written tests, or merely by reading, to deal realistically with administrative practice and problems, or even to educate in that evaluation of factors which every administrator must make and which is of the essence of his art in arriving at the equations through which he solves his problems.

Controversy on such questions goes far beyond the field of either Local Government or Central. Industry shows no clear pattern of thought or practice. Industrial practice does, however, reveal a growing tendency, and it is one favourable to the practice of Local Government: administrators and managers are increasingly drawn from those who possess a basic professional or technical training, and who, as they work up the ladder, acquire administrative or managerial experience and at some stage orientate their work to the administrative function.

The Professional Qualification

So far from burking any of the questions raised with regard to the requirement of professional qualification in the Local Government Service, we propose to review them a little more fully. Let us first, however, consider some of the factors which have led to the establishment of this requirement, after which we shall review the practice of the Local Authorities in the appointments they make at the higher administrative level.

The requirements for professional qualifications can partly be accounted for on historical grounds. The tasks with which modern Local Government began were largely of an executive character, and beyond all doubt the primary need of the Local Authorities in recruiting officers they could place in executive charge was for professional men. At the very outset, it should be noted, there was thus a contrast between the needs of the Local Authority and the needs of the Central Government, since the task of the latter did not extend to very much in the way of direct provision, but rather to functions of control and regulation, and was thus to be conceived of as administrative in character rather than executive. The balance is not quite the same to-day, but it is still true to say that the rôle of Local Government in the State is still preponderantly an executive one. It has the larger need, in fact, for professional staff. In looking at the Local Authority's domestic arrangements for the discharge of its task, either then or now, one sees a dividing line between staff with administrative and staff with executive functions, but what is equally apparent is that the need for officers in administrative command is, after all, very limited. Those participating in the administrative function may be numerous; those in administrative command are, and will continue to be, few.

In the last analysis administration at high level is itself only a product of the scale and complexity of organization. The very need for administration, and all its major problems,

N

spring essentially from the conditions set up by the division of labour involved in executive tasks of large scale and varied character. It is in fact the far-reaching division of labour involved in large-scale tasks which give rise to the administrator's essential tasks of organization, co-ordination, control, direction, and leadership. When, therefore, the Local Authority's functions had not attained either the vast scale or the great variety which they attain to-day, and while the tasks of Local Government were developing piece-meal, and no one could foresee the wide ambit they would reach, the primary need of the Local Authorities continued to be for staff with professional qualifications. They felt that the professional qualifications of the Clerk, the Treasurer or the Engineer could be relied upon for that modicum of administrative competence necessary to run departments of no vast magnitude. The need for co-ordination of a complex departmental machinery had hardly arisen.

In the larger Authorities this picture would no doubt change towards the end of the last century. The need for the administrator who could handle the big and complex machine would about then be arising. Whence were the administrators to be drawn? There was no intake from the universities. Neither the prestige of the Service nor the conditions within it were such as to attract graduates with the older kind of degree, had the Local Authorities thought that a likely quarter, *prima facie*, in which to find administrators. On the other hand, the authorities had within the ranks of their existing staffs professional men who had already acquired experience of the new administrative needs. These had hardly a rival in any other class of officer within the Service, since the educational standards of the clerical classes were then, as we have seen, deplorably low.

After the turn of the century, when the activities of Local Government expanded still more widely, and particularly during the inter-war years when the Local Authorities were called upon to pioneer so many of the new medical and social services, the picture would change still more. All except the more diminutive Local Authorities became

organisms of some size and variety which called for administrative command; but not even then had many of the
conditions which faced the Local Authorities in meeting
the situation materially changed. The intake of professional
staff had to be increased, and the variety of professional
staff engaged was wider than ever. The professional staffs
were still the greatest reservoir of mental training to be
found in the Service; and the degree of organization was
calling upon a proportion of them to orientate their activities
to the administrative side. Nor should it be overlooked that
the professional men in a large organization are bound to
acquire some knowledge and sense of the administrative
machine. On all these considerations it would have taken a
lot to convince the Local Authorities that any external
claimants to higher administrative posts could outweigh the
resources they already stood possessed of in a layer of professional officers with administrative functions, either in level of
mental capacity, knowledge of the work, or acquaintance
with the administrative environment in which it was to be
carried out.

Rightly or wrongly, the Local Authorities have continued
to rely upon these resources. It may be a paradox, but it is
nevertheless a fact, that in the last twenty years in which
the question has so frequently been posed as to whether
Local Authority practice should not allow of more freedom of access to the higher administrative posts, the hold
of the professional officers over appointments at this level
has in fact been consolidated. As chief officers in smaller
Authorities, often possessing no qualification whatever, have
retired on superannuation, their employing Councils have
almost invariably called for professional qualifications in the
appointment of their successors.

Administrative Experience

Whether the Local Authorities be right or wrong in relying
on professional staff for the pool from which administrators
can be chosen for higher office, there is no doubt to-day that
they do recognize the primary qualification for these higher
offices to be administrative capacity and experience. This is

the position to-day with even the medium-sized authorities, for even these are organisms of some complexity and size. It is seldom, if ever, that advertisements for these higher offices omit to stress the administrative requirements. And a similar statement is true of the advertisements for their deputies, and in large Authorities their chief assistants. The administrative requirements were stressed by the Hadow Committee, particularly in the case of the Clerk; and it was that committee which recommended that the Clerk should be regarded as the principal administrative officer—a sound recommendation in itself since even the minimum functions of the Clerk as secretary involve the more rudimentary elements of the administrative function, for reasons we indicated in Chapter II. The recommendations of the Hadow Committee, however, did but set the seal of approval upon the sense of values which most Local Authorities had themselves already developed, and which is now formally expressed in the designations they have approved for the Town Clerk and the other departmental heads, as mentioned in Chapter IV.

How do the administrative requirements come into the reckoning when the Local Authority is making an appointment of chief officer? The administrative experience it has to draw upon, whether in considering candidates from its own staff, or those who compete from among the staffs of other Authorities—and in these days a Local Authority rarely appoints without open competition of this kind—is built up in the following way. The young professional man will at first be engaged on purely professional work, and if, as is usually the case, he has acquired it by service with several Authorities, so much wider is his general knowledge of affairs as well as his professional experience. Even at this stage in his career duties of supervision and attendance with his principal at committee meetings, when matters he is handling come forward, will be giving him some sense of the mechanisms of administration. When these assistants move to the office of deputy (and in large Authorities, chief assistant), whether by promotion or by selection from among competing candidates from several Authorities, their duties will be substantially orientated to the administrative side, by way of assistance to the chief. An experienced deputy in a large Authority receives, in fact, very substantial delegations in the administrative sphere, under which he exercises a large measure of administrative command, subject to keeping his chief 'in touch', while the chief gets on with that block of Local Authority business which he chooses for direct personal attention.

Bearing in mind the width of the field of choice from competing candidates, these conditions, taken by and large, obviously secure a fair flow of administrative experience in the professional grades. The system is, of course, not infallible. Local Authorities are sometimes inclined to exaggerate the importance of peculiar local conditions, and of familiarity with them, and are thus led to promote one of their own staff in the face of the greater width and variety of experience which could be found in some outside candidate. Other things being equal, there is much to be said for giving preference to someone they know and someone who has secured their confidence; something to be said, too, from the general standpoint of staff relationships, in showing consideration to a member of their own staff and making an appointment which will encourage the staff as a whole and open up promotion 'down the line'. There is a certain danger, however, that these sentiments may lead to the preferment of a local man whose actual administrative experience has been short, e.g. when the vacancy occurs through the unexpected death of a principal officer, or his success in securing another appointment. The sentiment has sometimes led to the promotion of assistants almost fresh from purely professional work. A succession of such happenings has indeed been known to lead assistant solicitors into the highest office in county or city in the space of a few years, leaving some doubt in the mind of observers as to the maturity of their administrative training or experience. On the other hand, some, if not all, such appointments have fully proved themselves, large as the risk seemed to be which the Authority were taking. They have proved that the Local Authority knew their man.

In the foregoing review we have accorded the fullest force to the argument that the highest offices call primarily for administrative ability and experience. Apart, however, from the consideration that the appointment of professional men can secure considerable economy to the Local Authority in saving the fees of outside practitioners, quite a respectable argument can be put forward for the combination of professional and administrative experience. There is indeed some warrant in the experience gained in other spheres of administration for the virtues of such a combination. It means that the head of a department understands the work of his professional subordinates, even though he does not do it. It means that through the early exercise of a profession he has already acquired habits of judgment, made contacts with men and affairs, and had some experience of the kind of difficulty that crops up in administration continually and springs from human relationships in the discharge of a given task. In the case of local Government these considerations are reinforced by one slightly more specific; it is perhaps only in the very largest Authorities that the head of a department can in fact divorce himself from all concern with professional and technical work. And if a layman is appointed to a departmental headship, then, however brilliant, or whatever his background, there must in some measure always be a divorce in control as between the administrative and the professional sides. A lay-head has to 'take it' from his professional assistants, whereas the professional head can probe a little more deeply into the advice tendered to him.

From other quarters, however, there sometimes comes an argument that the mental disciplines involved in training for certain professions are positively disabling for the task of administration. On analysis the argument is usually seen to rest upon the particular rather than the general, and to be prompted by some of the more glaring 'mistakes' of the present system—errors in actual selection, instances of lawyers or doctors appointed to administrative command without administrative flair, and in some cases, perhaps, showing little interest in the administrative side of their duties.

It is said, for example, that the legal training of Town Clerks tends to make them unduly meticulous; and that their very virtues of wanting to assess every possible fact and argument in a doubtful situation make them hesitant and indecisive. Most Town Clerks would answer that so many things still remain obscure in Local Government law that they are continually called upon to take risks, and that sooner or later they learn to take them quite cheerfully. In the old days, the type of Town Clerk who reminds one of the pettifogging attorney may have survived in Local Government; but he does not, generally speaking, survive to-day. There is surely nothing in law which is a disabling training for the administrator—at any rate, the administrator who is free from eccentricities in temperament which should have precluded his appointment. To read law, after all, is to acquire a vast even if indirect acquaintance with the whole field of human nature and human relationships, and that surely is a background very relevant to the sphere of administration. Apart from this, it should be noted that the training of the solicitor is not quite so exclusively legal as that of the barrister, or so theoretic as that of the graduate in laws of a university, but extends to the many matters of business on which the average client expects his solicitor to be able to advise. It can indubitably provide a realistic knowledge of the ways of human beings and a useful insight into the nature and range of their affairs. It is difficult to see that such a training is not of value to the administrator-clerk.

If present practice could be proved to be leading to an inadequate supply of professional men with administrative experience, and if it could be reasonably demonstrated that there is some fund of ability and experience which could serve the Local Authority's needs better, the arguments against the present system would be much stronger than they are; but by and large matters do not seem to have got to that stage. It is fair, however, to notice one further argument against present practice. It is, in fact, the one used by the Hadow Committee, i.e. that the present practice may exclude the best. There is, as we have seen, no legal general prescription of professional qualifications; and no specific one at all for the highest office of all, i.e. that of Clerk. It is possible that the new administrative examination, if it achieves its contemplated standard, may throw up additional pools of ability in the administrative grades, supplemented in time perhaps by some infusion of university graduates. To throw up an alternative or an additional source of recruitment is all to the good if equivalent standards are maintained, but there is no sign as yet that there is any serious competitor, not, be it noted once more, to the professional man as such, but to the professional man who enters the Service and makes his way upward through professional and administrative strata in the way that we have described.

The arguments against present practice lay most emphasis on one particular office—that of the Clerk. No one has yet explored the virtues of appointing lawyers to be Borough Treasurers, and at the moment there is a legal obstacle in the way of appointing them to the office of Medical Officer of Health, but quite a lot of writers on Local Government have put forward the idea that there should be no reason why the Borough Treasurer or the Borough Engineer should not be considered a suitable candidate for the office of Town Clerk. A successful instance of this kind which they often cite is the appointment some years ago of the Education Officer to the Clerkship of the London County Council. In the majority of Local Authorities the argument may be decided by their view as to the extent to which even departmental heads must keep in touch with the professional aspect of the department's work, and on this we have said a word or two in a preceding paragraph. It is more difficult to resist the argument when the organization is of such a size that the Clerk must completely divorce himself from legal work. There is in fact no need to resist the argument at all; let there be the widest choice; the main stream of supply will still be what it is in the vast majority of cases.

Supplementary Training

Nothing that can be said in favour of the basic professional qualification should obscure the desirability—
perhaps the necessity—of supplementing it. The highest
offices in Local Authority employ call for wide mental
background; and for the office of Clerk, in particular, it is
not asking too much to call for some attested study and
knowledge of subjects in the field of social and political
science, economics, and comparative administration. For
those who aspire to be Town Clerks in the future the new
administrative qualification of the Local Government
Examination Board, and if not that, a Degree or Diploma in
Public Administration, should, if it attains the right standard, be quite an appropriate supplement to the legal
qualification. It may be asking too much in these times
to call for the double qualification on entry; but post-entry
training is not to be conceived of merely as a provision for
the lower levels of the Service. There is no less need for
it nearer the top. As for the Town Clerks of to-day, it is to
be hoped that they will orientate their Society to the function and status of a 'learned society'. There are signs that
they are doing so; but they have a long way to go yet in
following the enterprising example of the Treasurers in the
work which these officers do through their institute.

Conclusions

We can now summarize our conclusions as follows. Some
types of basic qualification may be better than others,
according to the particular field of administration. Perhaps
the chief and common virtue of them all, if they are of
fairly equivalent standard, is that, though they do not
make the administrator, they furnish the raw material from
which he is made, by producing that ' mental training '
which is so essential an ingredient in his composition.
Training for professional qualifications is as capable of
providing this mental training as university courses; and in
the Local Government Service it has been found to fit in
with the specific requirements for Local Government work.

It could well be supplemented by other 'administrative' qualifications of the type we have mentioned, normally by post-entry study. These administrative qualifications may in themselves eventually promote the supply of additional groups of personnel from which appointments to higher office can be made. A similar result could follow upon an infusion of university graduates into the subordinate levels of the Service, as was contemplated by the Charter; though the intake and the level of entry will require careful adjustment and regulation to safeguard the opportunities of promotion for serving staff who take qualifications by post-entry study. But neither of these new streams of supply for higher appointments seems likely to take the place of the professional stream. The Local Government Service is not likely to follow the Civil Service model in establishing a segregated higher administrative class by direct recruitment from the universities. On the other hand, it is safe to say that if the basic qualification remains predominantly the professional one, both the sentiment of the staffs and their employers will create an impetus towards the provision of the fullest facilities for acquiring professional qualifications by post-entry study. Questions of supply apart, post-entry study at all levels must be the main resource of the Service in responding to the call for efficiency in changing tasks and conditions. It will be a line of advance much in keeping with Service effort in the past, and much in keeping with current trends in every sphere. If the 'liberal education' in the older tradition still has its incomparable values, it is no longer regarded as a universal and immediate passport to the upper levels of responsibility and control. We may be moving to some new form of an old conception—work and training in combination. It has, in all ages and societies, been a fruitful one in the growth and advance of human skills of every kind.

Epilogue

ON SOME topics introduced into the foregoing pages it would have been possible to say much more. Our references to administration, and to the administrative officer, could have been rounded off with some discussion of the administrative function and of the personal qualities which go to make up the administrator. A fuller treatment of Local Authority practice and standards in the selection of staff—particularly for the higher appointments—would have been welcomed by some readers. And, in the chapters just concluded, what is said about training in the wider sense seems sketchy in comparison with the fuller treatment of qualifications.

But something must be sacrificed in a short work; and the foregoing pages must be judged in the light of the aims and themes put forth in the Introduction. If they have fulfilled these aims they will have shown the reader that the Local Government Service is truly a Service in the sense which has become attached to that term, one which makes available a rich store of varied skills and experience to the elected representatives of the people, and places in their hands an indispensable and efficient instrument for their task of meeting fundamental human needs. They will have given the reader some idea of the tasks the Service performs and the standards it observes and attains in performing them; some idea, too, of the effort which it has taken to establish these standards, and of the continuing effort which is being made to maintain and improve these standards. They will, it is hoped, have shown the reader how vital to his interests as a citizen the maintenance of an efficient Local Government Service is; and how important, from his own point of view, is all the work, largely unseen, but difficult and complex, that is being carried out with this object by the several agencies we have described. And if these pages have succeeded in showing all this, the main purpose of this book will have been achieved.

There is one question on which we have said hardly anything—the adequacy or otherwise of the remuneration of Local Government officers; and it is one on which readers who are members or officers of local authorities will have thought our reticence strange. In a book such as this it would have been improper to embark upon any discussion of matters relating to pay which are in issue at present, and being dealt with by the appropriate agencies; and in any event any appraisement of pay standards would reach a length and complexity beyond the compass of a work such as this. Something may be said, however, in conclusion, on the principles which enter into the determination of the remuneration of such public servants as Local Government officers.

No completely satisfactory formula has yet been found. In an introduction to the Charter signed by the Independent Chairman and the Chairman of the two Sides, agreement was expressed with a 'Fair Wages principle'—that Local Government should not take the lead in determining salary standards but should be 'in the first flight of good employers'. Mr. Ernest Bevin, when Minister of Labour, acknowledged in the course of a Parliamentary discussion that in his experience as a trade-union officer, the policy of the Treasury had been, not to be model employers, but to pay standard rates. As we incidentally said in Chapter II, public servants cannot expect the glittering prizes of the commercial world, or expect to be paid at rates continuously related to the level of the most flourishing businesses, while avoiding all comparison with the less flourishing, and escaping the risks of less stable forms of employment.

The nearest approach to a formula was the short rubric propounded by the Tomlin Commission on the Civil Service —that remuneration in the public service should follow the 'long-term trend' in outside occupations. One implication of this is that service pay cannot be continually adjusted to meet fluctuations in the more elastic market conditions outside. Thus broadly stated, the doctrine has some force. If remuneration is to be regulated by the system of gradings and incremental scales characteristic of pay arrangements in

the public services, there are obvious limitations to adjustments during the 'life' of the scales. The doctrine also
affords some safeguards to the staffs; for if transient fluctuations are to be ruled out it follows that the public services
should not be penalized in a 'slump' if they have not
participated in the fruits of a 'boom'.

But however just the Tomlin formula was in 'normal'
times, it requires to be applied with more elasticity in times
like the present. The present times are not 'normal', nor
have they been almost at any time since the Tomlin Commission (1934). The intervals for adjustment must be more
frequent in conditions when the 'long-term' trend is itself
moving at a greater pace than it used to do, and when the
cost of living increases steeply in a comparatively short space
of time, and 'outside' earnings make a concurrent if not a
fully compensating upward movement, as has happened in
the post-war years. In short, if the Tomlin formula is to
retain any cogency and equity, the quantitative interpretation of 'long-term' must be different from that which was in
the minds of the Tomlin Commission at the time. Recent
conditions, too, have brought out a factor which, if it was
implicit in the formula, must be given a new emphasis, and,
if it was not, must be used to supplement it, i.e. the ruling
levels of pay in the public services must be such as to attract
and retain staff of the necessary ability, qualifications and
experience for work which must be carried out to meet
vital public needs. There is some evidence that both the
Civil Service and the Local Government Service have
suffered some detriment in post-war years through the
very much more attractive conditions ruling outside;
particularly for staff with the higher qualifications and
responsibilities.

It is obviously no easy task for negotiators on one side or
the other to translate broad considerations such as those
above expressed into quantitative terms in the settlement of
salaries; even with the reasonable spirit and the sense of
overriding conditions which are the *sine qua non* in these tasks.

In the last analysis the pay and conditions of the Service
will be determined by the public sense of the importance of

Local Government, the work which Local Government officers do, and the standards of ability, education, qualification, training, and conduct which their work calls for. Staffs in public services will, we believe, be found to have been misguided, in the long run, if they resort to pressure campaigns or the cruder forms of propaganda in their address to the public mind; but they are fully entitled to keep the public mind informed as to the importance and character of their responsibilities, as in fact Local Government officers do through a very important side of the work of N.A.L.G.O. But, having said this, we make bold to say that they are not likely to find any better methods or machinery for the settlement of their conditions of contract, and the adjustment of their relationships with their employers, than those of the Whitleyism they have so largely built up by their own prolonged effort.

APPENDIX A
CHARTER SCALES (1951)
(*Exclusive of "London Weighting"*)
GENERAL DIVISION

Age		MALES Salary £	Annual Increment £		FEMALES Salary £	Annual Increment £
16	......	150	15	......	120	12
17	......	165	15	......	132	12
18	......	180	20	......	144	16
19	......	200	20	......	160	16
20	......	220	25	......	176	20
21	......	245	25	......	196	20
22	......	270	20	......	216	16
23	......	290	20	......	232	16
24	......	310	25	......	248	20
25	......	335	25	......	268	20
26	......	360	20	......	288	16
27	......	380	20	......	304	16
28	......	400	10	......	320	8
29	......	410	15	......	328	12
30	......	425	—	......	340	—

CLERICAL DIVISION

MALES Salary £	Annual Increment £		FEMALES Salary £	Annual Increment £
445	15	......	356	12
460	15	......	368	12
475	15	......	380	12
490	—	......	392	—

HIGHER CLERICAL DIVISION

MALES Salary £	Annual Increment £		FEMALES Salary £	Annual Increment £
490	15	......	394	12
505	15	......	406	12
520	15	......	418	12
535	—	......	430	—

ADMINISTRATIVE, PROFESSIONAL AND TECHNICAL DIVISION

MALES AND FEMALES

Salary £	Annual Increment £	Salary £	Annual Increment £
GRADE I		GRADE V(a)	
440	15	600	20
455	15	620	20
470	15	640	20
485	—	660	—
GRADE II		GRADE VI	
470	15	645	20
485	15	665	20
500	15	685	25
515	—	710	—
GRADE III		GRADE VII	
500	15	685	25
515	15	710	25
530	15	735	25
545	—	760	—
GRADE IV		GRADE VIII	
530	15	735	25
545	15	760	25
560	15	785	25
575	—	810	—
GRADE V		GRADE IX	
570	15	790	40
585	15	830	40
600	20	870	40
620	—	910	—

GRADE X

Salary £	Annual Increment £
870	40
910	40
950	50
1,000	—

MISCELLANEOUS DIVISION
(Governed by Supplementary Scheme)

APPENDIX B

SCALES FOR TOWN AND DISTRICT COUNCIL CLERKS

(Under Recommendations of Negotiating Commitee "A"— 8th September, 1949)

Population*	Salary Ranges		Annual Increments
(1)	(2) £	(3) £	(4)
(1) Under 5,000	500–650	650–800	3 of £50
(2) 5/10,000	700–850	850–1,000	3 of £50
(3) 10/15,000	800–1,000	1,000–1,200	4 of £50
(4) 15/20,000	1,000–1,200	1,200–1,400	4 of £50
(5) 20/30,000	1,150–1,350	1,350–1,550	4 of £50
(6) 30/45,000	1,350–1,550	1,550–1,750	4 of £50
(7) 45/60,000	1,500–1,750	1,750–2,000	5 of £50
(8) 60/75,000	1,750–2,000	2,000–2,250	2 of £100, 1 of £50
(9) 75/100,000	2,000–2,250	2,250–2,500	2 of £100, 1 of £50
(10) 100/150,000	2,250–2,500	2,500–2,750	2 of £100, 1 of £50
(11) 150/250,000	2,500–2,750	2,750–3,000	2 of £100, 1 of £50
(12) 250/400,000	2,750–3,000	3,000–3,250	2 of £100, 1 of £50
(13) 400/600,000	3,000–3,250	3,250–3,500	2 of £100, 1 of £50
(14) Over 600,000	At discretion		

Interpretation

A Local Authority within a population group set out in column (1) hereof shall pay their Clerk a salary commencing at a figure within the limits indicated in column (2) and proceeding to a maximum within the limits indicated in column (3) by annual increments of the number and value set out in column (4).

In view of their special circumstances, the Cities of London and Westminster shall be treated, for the purpose of this Schedule, in the same way as those Authorities who have a population exceeding 600,000 persons.

In deciding the position of their Clerk within the foregoing ranges, the Council should have regard to the factors mentioned in paragraph 4 in the preamble and to such other local factors, if any, as appear to them to be relevant.

Upon the initial application of these terms by the Council, the Council shall have regard to the length of service of the Clerk as Clerk of the Council when placing him in an appropriate place within the salaries scale selected.

*According to the latest estimate for the time being of the Registrar-General.

N.B. Paragraph 4 in the preamble to the agreement mentions specifically the following factors—varying responsibilities of different classes of authorities or their officers even where population levels may be the same, 'areas in or around London where expenses are usually higher,' holiday resorts and inland spas in which there are large seasonal influxes of visitors, areas where the Clerk is also financial officer, and areas (especially in the lower population categories) where a legally qualified clerk is employed.

APPENDIX C

SCALES FOR ACCOUNTANTS AND TREASURERS, ENGINEERS AND SURVEYORS, CHIEF EDUCATION OFFICERS, AND ARCHITECTS IN CHARGE OF SEPARATE DEPARTMENTS

(Under Recommendations of Committee " B " dated 12th September, 1950)

Population (1)	Minimum salary (2)	Increments (3)	
Not exceeding 5,000	Between £450 and £600	3 of £50	
5/10,000	,, £600 ,, £750	3 of £50	
10/15,000	,, £600 ,, £850	3 of £50	
15/20,000	,, £750 ,, £1,000	3 of £50	
20/30,000	,, £800 ,, £1,100	3 of £50	
30/45,000	,, £900 ,, £1,300	4 of £50	
45/60,000	,, £1,050 ,, £1,450	4 of £50	
60/75,000	,, £1,250 ,, £1,650	4 of £50	
75/100,000	,, £1,350 ,, £1,850	5 of £50	
100/150,000	,, £1,550 ,, £2,050	5 of £50	
150/250,000	,, £1,750 ,, £2,250	2 of £100.	1 of £50.
250/400,000	,, £2,000 ,, £2,500	2 of £100.	1 of £50.
400/600,000	,, £2,100 ,, £2,700	3 of £100.	
Over 600,000	at discretion		

Interpretation

A Local Authority within a population group set out in column (1) shall fix for each chief officer a salary scale commencing at a figure within the limits indicated in column (2) and proceeding by the annual increments set out in column (3) to a maximum determined by the number and value of those increments. *An Authority need not necessarily pay each chief officer a salary upon the same scale.* Each Local Authority should decide in the light of local circumstances the question whether the Treasurer, Engineer, Chief Education Officer and Architect should be remunerated on the same or on different scales.

In view of their special circumstances, the Cities of London and Westminster shall be treated, for the purpose of this Schedule, in the same way as those Authorities who have a population exceeding 600,000 persons.

In deciding the scales to be adopted, the Council should have regard to the factors mentioned in paragraph 4 in the preamble and to such other local factors, if any, as appear to them to be relevant.

Upon the initial application of these terms by the Council, the Council shall have regard to the length of service of the officer as chief officer when placing him at an appropriate place within the scale selected.

N.B. Article 4 in the preamble to the agreement mentions the same factors as were mentioned in the agreement for Clerks, etc., except those relating to the case where the Clerk is also Financial Officer, and to the possession of a legal qualification.

APPENDIX D

A Select Bibliography

I. Historical

From Patronage to Proficiency in the Public Service, by W. A. Robson; 1922; Fabian Tract.

The First Report of the Committee on Relations between Employers and Employed (*The Whitley Report*), 1917.

Final Report of the Royal Commission on Local Government 1929-30, Vol. XV.

Report of the Departmental Committee on the Qualifications, Training, Recruitment and Promotion of Local Government Officers (*The Hadow Report*), 1934.

The Local Government Officer, by L. Hill; 1938; Allen & Unwin (O.P.).

Chapter VI: " The Municipal Service," *A Century of Municipal Progress,* by L. Hill; 1935; Allen & Unwin (O.P.).

II. Works on Local Government

English Local Government: by H. Finer; revised fourth edition, 1950; Methuen; 36s.

The English Local Government System, by J. H. Warren; revised second edition, 1950; Allen & Unwin; 7s. 6d.

Municipal Administration, by J. H. Warren; 1948; Pitman, 15s.

The Development of Local Government, by W. A. Robson; revised second edition, 1948; Allen & Unwin; 18s.

For reference: *The Encyclopaedia of Local Government Law and Administration,* edited by Lord Macmillan; 14 vols. and cumulative supplements; Butterworth & Co.

III. Current Documents

National Joint Council for Local Authorities' Administrative, Professional, Technical and Clerical Services.

(*a*) National Scheme of Conditions of Service (The Charter)
(*b*) Scheme of Service Conditions for Miscellaneous Classes.
(*c*) Constitution of the National Joint Council.
(*d*) Model Constitution for Provincial Councils.
(*e*) Model Constitution for Local Joint Committees.

Negotiating Committees—" A " for Clerks to Local Authorities and " B " for other Chief Officers and Officers above £1,000 per annum.

Recommendations as to Conditions of Service and Scales of Salaries.

Local Government Examinations Board
  (*a*) Constitution and Functions
  (*b*) Regulations and Syllabus for (1) the former Promotion Examination, (2) the Clerical Examination, and (3) the Administrative Examination (Intermediate and Final).
  (*c*) Lists of alternative Examinations.
  (*d*) Annual Reports.
  (*e*) 'Examinations for Promotion'; price 6d. (This booklet now brings together current Regulations, Syllabus, etc.)

National Association of Local Government Officers
  Brochures on Superannuation, Compensation, Legal Protection, etc.
  Report of the General Secretary on the question of Affiliation to the Trades Union Congress (1948).
  Report and Scheme for Adaptation of the Association's Machinery (1950).

Institute of Public Administration
  Establishment Work in Local Authorities: Conference papers and reports, 1949 (10s.) and 1950 (7s. 6d.).

  Local Government Establishment Work—published for the Institute by Allen and Unwin, 1951; 7s. 6d.

  N.B. Not all the foregoing documents are on sale in the usual ways, but within reasonable limits copies may be made available to students and research workers on application to the appropriate secretariats: Local Authorities Conditions of Service Advisory Board (for National Joint Council, Local Government Examinations Board, and Negotiating Committees A and B), 37 Upper Grosvenor Street, London, W.1.; National Association of Local Government Officers, 1 York Gate, Regent's Park, London, N.W.1.

Index

215

For Product Safety Concerns and Information please contact our EU
representative GPSR@taylorandfrancis.com
Taylor & Francis Verlag GmbH, Kaufingerstraße 24, 80331 München, Germany

www.ingramcontent.com/pod-product-compliance
Lightning Source LLC
Chambersburg PA
CBHW070241290326
41929CB00046B/2299